CASE STUDIES IN
CULTURAL ANTHROPOLOGY

GENERAL EDITORS
George and Louise Spindler
STANFORD UNIVERSITY

DREAMERS WITHOUT POWER

The Menomini Indians

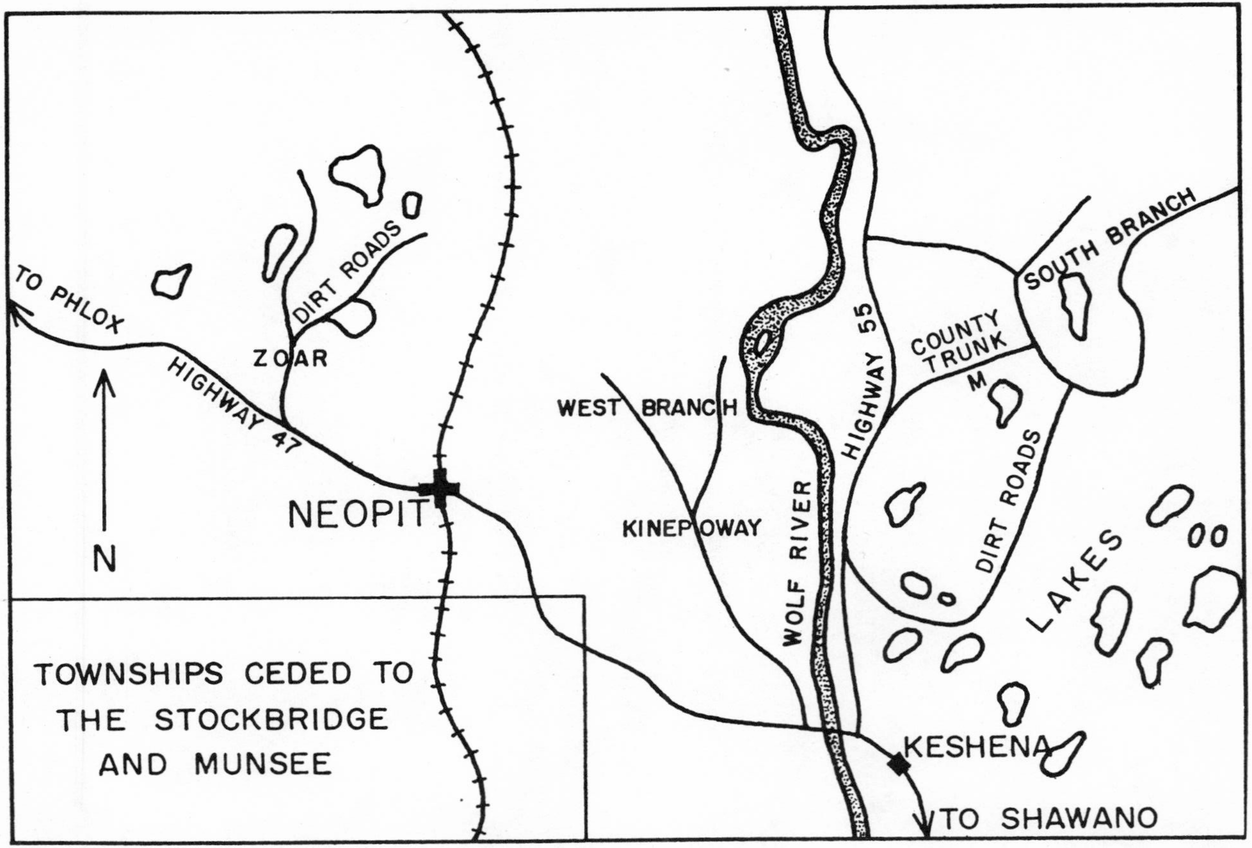

Menominee County

TO SHAWANO

KESHENA

LAKES

SOUTH BRANCH

COUNTY TRUNK M

DIRT ROADS

HIGHWAY 55

WOLF RIVER

WEST BRANCH

KINEPOWAY

NEOPIT

DIRT ROADS

ZOAR

HIGHWAY 47

TO PHLOX

N

TOWNSHIPS CEDED TO THE STOCKBRIDGE AND MUNSEE

DREAMERS
WITHOUT POWER
The Menomini Indians

By

GEORGE SPINDLER AND LOUISE SPINDLER

Stanford University

1971

HOLT, RINEHART AND WINSTON, INC.

NEW YORK CHICAGO SAN FRANCISCO ATLANTA
DALLAS MONTREAL TORONTO LONDON SYDNEY

This book is dedicated to the
MENOMINI PEOPLE
and to our family
SUE, LLOYD, VICKI, AND REBECCA

Cover photos: *(1) Dewey Wynoss dances at Beartrap Falls near Keshena in 1952 with costumes and dance movements in the authentic woodlands style; (2) Menomini leave a general council meeting.*

Copyright © 1971 by Holt, Rinehart and Winston, Inc.
All rights reserved
Library of Congress Catalog Card Number: 75–146450
SBN: 03—085542—x
Printed in the United States of America
1 2 3 4   059   9 8 7 6 5 4 3 2 1

Foreword

About the Series

These case studies in cultural anthropology are designed to bring to students, in beginning and intermediate courses in the social sciences, insights into the richness and complexity of human life as it is lived in different ways and in different places. They are written by men and women who have lived in the societies they write about and who are professionally trained as observers and interpreters of human behavior. The authors are also teachers, and in writing their books they have kept the students who will read them foremost in their minds. It is our belief that when an understanding of ways of life very different from one's own is gained, abstractions and generalizations about social structure, cultural values, subsistence techniques, and the other universal categories of human social behavior become meaningful.

About the Authors

George and Louise Spindler began fieldwork with the Menomini as graduate students in anthropology at the University of Wisconsin in 1948. It was their major professional preoccupation for more than a decade, and they have maintained continuous contact with the Menomini to the present. The book is a fully collaborative product. Each has used freely the field notes, unpublished writings, and published works of the other. The writing was done in their home in the forest close to the boundary of Menomini lands. While writing, they had the opportunity to check out facts and ideas with some of the Menomini themselves.

George Spindler is professor of anthropology and education at Stanford University, and Louise Spindler is research associate and lecturer in the department of anthropology. They edited the *American Anthropologist* from 1962 to 1966 and are editors of the series in which this book and others appear. George Spindler holds a Ph.D. from the University of California at Los Angeles, with a major in cultural anthropology and minors in psychology and sociology. Louise Spindler holds a Ph.D. from Stanford University in cultural anthropology. Both are fellows of the American Anthropological Association. The Spindlers have done fieldwork with the Menomini, Blood, and Mistassini Cree Indians and in rural Germany. George Spindler has worked intermittently for several years in United States school systems. They have published various articles and monographs on some of the results of their research.

About the Book

This book is a study of the final phases of adaptation of the Menomini Indians of Wisconsin to the results of the confrontation between their way of life and the ways of the Whiteman. It is the story of a people who existed in a cognitive world radically different from that of the West. The Menomini were dreamers and people of power. Their religious associations, rituals, witch bags, and medicine bundles were all devices for acquiring and maintaining sacred power. Their dreams told them of the future, instructed them about the meaning of events, gave them roles and purposes in life, and provided them with access to power. Today only a few still dream, and only a very few still have sacred power.

The Menomini are a very small minority group with a place in the United States of America, in the State of Wisconsin, called Menominee County.[1] They are struggling to survive. Beset by financial problems of staggering magnitude, rent by internal factionalism, they are doing the best they can. The Menomini reservation, one of the few nearly self-sufficient tribal communities under the protection and guarantees of the federal government, was terminated, as this protection and these guarantees were withdrawn, on May 1, 1961, after years of painful negotiations. The termination has proven to be expensive to the State of Wisconsin and the United States as well as to the Menomini. Due to the efforts of the Menomini themselves and with the help of some good friends, there appears to be a chance that a Menomini community will survive into the future. If it does, it will be a very different kind of community than the Menomini themselves would recognize as related to their past cultural identity. The effects of termination and the prospects for the future are touched upon in the last chapter.

Most of the book is not about the adaptation to termination, which is only one aspect of the struggle for survival. It is about the several adaptive strategies which various segments of the Menomini have employed to cope with the prolonged confrontation between incongruent cultural systems—their own and the Whiteman's. We have described these strategies as native oriented, peyote, transitional, and acculturated. The major proportion of space is devoted to the first three, for they represent those being made while the influence of the traditional Menomini culture was still substantial. In this analysis we show how the chasm between Menomini culture and Western culture was almost untraversable, given the divergence between them.

This study is relevant, we think, to many places in the world where Western culture (particularly its American version) has confronted relatively powerless, divergent cultures. It is particularly relevant for understanding the relationship between non-European minorities in the United States and the dominant population of European and Anglo-Saxon derivation, as these minorities

---

[1] When referring to the present county and corporation, we have used the spelling "Menominee." "Menomini" has been used in most of the literature. We have used Menomini in referring to cultural process, present groups, and past history and Menominee in referring to the present county and the corporation (Menominee Enterprises, Inc.). As far as we know, the people themselves have never expressed a specific preference.

are struggling for full participation in the economic, political, and social life of this country. The analysis also has implications for understanding the consequences of other confrontations occurring today in our society, including, possibly, those between generations. One can find parallels to the native oriented, peyote, transitional, and acculturated adaptations among the non-Indian population of the United States.

To those who know of our research with the Menomini through previous publications, it may be of interest to know that we have included substantial amounts of previously unpublished material, and that the analysis, though it builds upon previous work, is a reinterpretation, as well as an extension, of previous works.

To both those who know some of our previous work and those who have no acquaintance with it, the chapter "Fieldwork with the Menomini" in *Being an Anthropologist: Fieldwork in Eleven Cultures*, edited by G. Spindler (1970), should be of interest. Since this chapter makes the methodology standing behind this book explicit, we have included only passing reference to methods in this already overextended case study.

To the students who read this case study, we want to say that we have violated some of the policies we have tried to implement, as editors of the Case Studies in Cultural Anthropology series, for other contributing authors. This case study is longer than most, and we have allowed ourselves to become involved with some relatively technical and theoretical matters that are ordinarily less emphasized in the case studies. We have also made some value judgments, most of them, hopefully, explicit. Our excuses for doing these things are all rationalizations, so we will not bother to state them. We have tried, however, to make everything as clear as we are capable of making it.

To the Menomini who read this book, we want to say that we know you will like some of it, dislike some of it, and find much of it irrelevant to your present crisis. We have often used your words in order to avoid superimposing our meaning on yours, but in the last analysis we are responsible for what is said here. We are in your debt for allowing us to observe you, question you, administer psychological tests to you, and enjoy ourselves with you and on your lands. We hope that the book casts prejudice on no one and that it may even do you some small good at this critical point in your history.[2]

GEORGE AND LOUISE SPINDLER
General Editors

---

[2] As a concrete manifestation of this hope, we are sharing the royalties from this book with the Menomini people.

Acknowledgments

Every author of every book incurs more debts than can be paid. Anthropologists and others who write about their fellow humans are doubly indebted, for whatever they write they learned from the people who are their subjects. We learned from literally hundreds of Menomini. We learned more from some than from others, of course, and we would like to name them. And yet to do so would somehow be unfair. Nor would it be in the best of the Menomini tradition. They shall go nameless, therefore, but we will always remember them with the deepest affection and gratitude.

There are some non-Menomini whom we can name who helped us in special ways. Julia Kringel saw to it that the manuscript was typed and sent, made numerous changes at our request, and now and then criticized what we wrote, to good effect. Fred Voget and Kalil Gezi read the entire manuscript, criticized, and encouraged. Though not responsible for what we wrote, they helped.

A special thanks goes to the many students at Stanford who have listened to us while we talked about the Menomini and who, by their interest and their questions, have stimulated us to broaden our interpretations.

Menomini Phonemes[1]

Consonants

	Labial	Dental	Alveolo-palatal	Mid-palatal	Glottal
Voiceless stops	p	t	c	k	ʔ
Voiceless fricatives			s		h
Voiced nasals	m	n			
Semivowels	w		y		

Vowels

	Front		Back	
	Short	Long	Short	Long
High	i	i·	u	u·
Mid	e	e·	o	o·
Low	ɛ	ɛ·	a	a·

[1] From Slotkin 1957.

Contents

DREAMERS WITHOUT POWER

The Menomini Indians

The sawmill from which, together with the associated lumber industry, most Menomini make their living.

One of the Dream Dance drums and the singers at an annual fall rite.

1

The Framework

In the beginning me·c-awe·tok, the Supreme God, created the world by putting islands into the great waters. Then he took up some earth like wax and moulded in his hand the image of a human being. Then he blew his breath four times upon it and it came to life and it was his son, Jesus. He placed him across the great waters on the other islands and old German country and gave them to him to protect and rule. Then the Supreme God took up red clay, made a tiny image and blew his breath upon it four times. The last time he blew life into the clay and made me?napos, his servant, to protect this island and his grandmother's people and he decreed that Jesus and me?napos should be friends and brothers, each to remain on his separate island and to take care of his people. All went well until Columbus crossed the ocean. . . . Then everything began to conflict so that now no one in this world can ever understand it.[1]

The Adaptation

THE MENOMINI are not today a single people, even though Menomini distinguish themselves not only from Whites, Blacks, Chicanos, and other non-Indians but also from other Indians. Many forces have torn the Menomini apart. They have made several distinctive adaptations to the demands and threats of the dominant American culture and society. The Menomini were confined over a century ago to a reservation (see p. ii) that was a fraction of the size of their original territory. They could no longer live by fishing, gathering wild rice, hunting, and marginal horticulture, though some continued to try to do so. The fur trade that they had come to depend upon collapsed during the first half of the nineteenth century. The Whiteman's[2] religion and education were presented as

---

[1] The beginning of a version of the birth of *Me?napos*, the Menomini culture hero, as told to Alanson Skinner (Skinner and Satterlee 1915:241).

[2] The term "Whiteman" is frequently used in this book to denote the dominant American cultural system as Menomini perceived and experienced it. This is the term they have used themselves.

1

exclusive channels to self-improvement, and to approval by the dominant White-man society. The Whiteman's technological and occupational system was the only set of instrumentalities that was productive in the changed setting, and the Menomini, for complex reasons, of which prejudice was only one, were denied anything resembling full-scale participation. Paradoxically, however, the Menomini, with the help of some astute White politicians, preserved the forest cover on part of their nearly 400 square miles of reservation long after the original forest had been ravaged elsewhere in the northcentral states, and it is from this forest that most of the Menomini today gain their livelihood, though in a very different manner than did their ancestors who once roamed the same forest. To all of these radical changes in the conditions of their existence, the Menomini have made adaptations.

The Consequences

Though the Menomini made these adaptations over a period of time, and neither their adaptations nor the conditions to which they adapted remained constant, there are certain consequences that remain in force today. There are, within the Menomini community, five major cultural divisions. The *native-oriented* group maintains the Dream Dance, called the *ni·mihe·twan* ("dancing rite") in the native language, the Medicine Lodge (the *mete·wen*), the War, or Chief's, Dance (*okeceta·we·ʔseman*), and other rituals, all "religious" in character.[3] In social interaction, and in the values, perceptions, and personalities of its members, recognizable though often attenuated patterns are functioning that appear to be of traditional derivation, modified to meet present conditions. The *Peyotists* are members of the Native American Church. Most were raised in culturally conservative households, at least through early childhood, and all have had substantial contact with Whiteman culture. Their rites include the eating of peyote, the bud of the cactus *Lophophera williamsii*, which has hallucinogenic properties. Though there is considerable antagonism between the native-oriented group and the Peyotists, members of both groups live in the same general area, interact with each other more than with others, and share a common cultural fund of belief and values. The *transitionals* include individuals loosely joined together in informal groupings, such as drinking groups, people who are almost wholly isolated, and people who are striving toward fuller participation in the non-Menomini world. It is a heterogeneous category. The people within it have in common early experience with traditional cultural forms, but they are people who have moved away from overt identification with the old culture and who are not participants in any traditional organization such as the *ni·mihe·twan* or any "nativistic" organization such as the Peyote church. Some of the transitionals exhibit signs of pathological social marginality in their behavior and uncertain identities, but not all do.[4] The *lower-*

---

[3] See "Menomini Phonemes," p. xi.

[4] We have not used the concept "marginal man" heavily in this book because we are wary of its implications. Marginality, as a product of the specific conditions existing for the Menomini, results in identity loss and personal and social disorder (see Chapter 4). When there is a positive support for more than one identity, however, as there could be in a truly pluralistic cultural system, and for several reference groups representing quite different affiliations, marginality may be productive, and even particularly satisfying.

Preparing a powwow for tourists, 1960.

Menomini leaving a general council meeting.

These traditional shelters were still in use near Zoar in 1953.

A new house (1969) in Neopit.

status acculturated are people who are overtly assimilated into Western culture and who are not members of traditional or nativistic groups. They differ from the *elite acculturated* in that their social and economic position is somewhat lower. The lower-status acculturated support themselves with jobs that, while by no means menial, are not management or professional positions. The elite acculturated can be regarded as the people who have, in whiteman terms, "made it." Included among them are entrepreneurs, men and women with supervisory positions in the lumbermill or associated enterprises, and skilled white-collar workers. There are no doctors or lawyers in the group, though no doubt there soon will be. There are also a number of people, mostly young, who have left the home community and are residing in Milwaukee, Chicago, and other large cities.

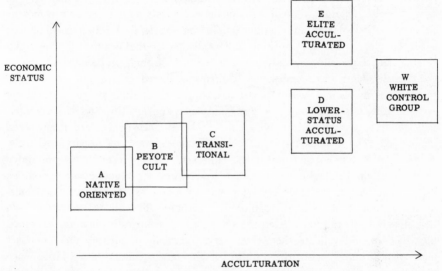

Figure 1. Acculturative categories.

These categories can be arranged in terms of their approximation to middle-Western cultural norms in the United States, and in relative economic rank. The placements on these two axes, acculturation and economic status, are given in Fig. 1. Their relative positions have been established statistically, using indexes such as occupation, education, household furnishings, display of native objects, language, and participation in religious activities, collected on a socio-cultural index schedule for each individual in our sample. We use the term "acculturative categories" to designate these groupings. We intend that acculturation should be thought of in its broad sense as adaptation by members of a cultural system to changes in the conditions of existence wrought by the impact of another upon it. The Menomini may be said to be acculturating to the impact of Western culture as represented by the whole gamut of personnel from French fur traders to nuns and priests and Antigo businessmen.[5] This process

---

[5] Antigo is a town of about 8000 population near the northwestern boundaries of the Menomini lands.

began in the early seventeenth century and is continuing today. We must keep in mind, however, that each of the acculturative categories is a unique adaptation to the confrontation between two very divergent cultural systems. Seen from that point of view, they do not represent a steady progression from "traditional" to "modern." They are all contemporary attempts to get along in a conflicting social, cultural, political, and personal environment.

The role of religion in these adaptations is of particular significance. The native-oriented group maintains the Dream Dance, Medicine Lodge, Chief's Dance, and various lesser rituals as a way of defining its existence and identity. The Peyotists have created a religion that resolves some of the conflict created by the confrontation of Whiteman and Menomini cultures. It serves to give them, as well, an identity, and, as in the case of all identities, it draws some boundaries between the group and others. The transitionals have no firm identity and no firm religious affiliation, though individuals within this large category are moving in various directions to an identity and in some cases to a religious affiliation: a few to a native-oriented position, others to that of the Whiteman. The acculturated, and especially the elite acculturated, are strongly Catholic and present the clearest identity as members of Whiteman-affiliated groups and cultural patterns. The symbols and behaviors characterizing each of these religious groupings serve to consolidate meanings, reaffirm allegiance and identity, and vitalize interpersonal relationships within the group. Acceptable self-images are formed and maintained. The demands of the cultural system and the instrumental roles provided within it are given validity. However, lest we seem to be committed to the position that religious affiliation *determines* acculturative adaptation, let us say that we see religious behavior and affiliation as symptomatic of fundamental economic as well as cognitive adaptations. Like all belief systems—in fact, like all of cultural patterning—they are teleological; once in existence, they reaffirm and validate themselves, serve functions of identity and boundary maintenance, and support the validity of the larger cultural system of which they are a part. It is important, too, to understand that affiliations other than religious, in the strict sense of the word, may provide many of these same functions—for example, strong commitment to political ideologies, particularly in the context of sociopolitical movements, as in the Red Power movement, may become significant determinants as well as expressions of new forms of adaptation. In any event, in this book, we are mostly concerned with the perceptual and cognitive manifestations of adaptation rather than with the institutional or role-adaptive processes.

To What Did They Adapt?

The Menomini are not to be seen as merely responding to the impact of Whiteman culture. They are and always have been adapting to the total environment, and they are a part of their own environment. They impute meanings, make decisions, and produce rationalizations for their behavior that become self-sustaining and constitute a part of the environment to which adaptation must

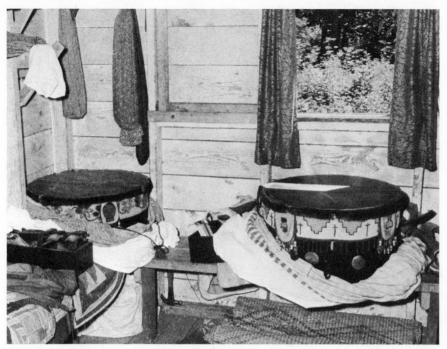

The Dream Dance drums are kept in a special place, with all the ritual paraphernalia. They are kept covered when not used (the covers were partially removed so we could take this picture). The beadwork around the top tells the story of the origin of the Dream Dance. A kerosene lamp is kept burning all night by them.

The Catholic church at Neopit.

be made. Nor are the Menomini dealing with some fixed, static, and certain cultural entity. The "American" culture to which they were adapting in 1854, when the reservation was created, is remarkably different from the American culture to which they are adapting today. Even during the span of our fieldwork with them, we have seen phenomenal changes in our own way of life.

Furthermore, the Menomini were never and are not now adapting to an abstract Western culture. They have adapted to the culture as represented by the people with whom they have come in direct contact—initially, missionaries, fur traders, and rum runners; later, priests, soldiers, and teachers, merchants and farmers, government agents, politicians and professionals, tourists, land developers, and owners of vacation homes. They have also adapted to a local northeastern Wisconsin culture that is still regionally distinctive, and quite different from, for instance, that of the peninsula area of northern California. They have adapted to this culture variously; some to its laboring-class segments, some to the culture of its farmers, some to the way of life of the middle class of its towns, and others to its deviant elements.

The Confrontation

Underlying the diversity of contacts, however, there appear to be certain massive and very pervasive differences between Menomini culture and Western culture in all its particularistic manifestations that have made it extremely difficult for most of the Menomini to make a viable adaptation *as Menomini*. The orientations toward reality, the assumptions about what a person should be like, or even what a person is, are so divergent that there seems to have been no way to synthesize the two cultures. There has been no way to be a Menomini Indian and Whiteman at the same time, given the criteria for acceptance and participation applied by the latter to the former, and given the pervasive cultural discongruity that we will discuss. It has been much more difficult, in any event, to be a "successful" (that is, functional) Menomini-American that it has been to be a successful Irish-American, Italian-American, or even Japanese-American.

Two qualifying statements must be made: (1) This clearly does not mean that people of Menomini descent cannot be "good" Americans (it does mean that they have rarely been able to remain *culturally* Menomini while becoming and being "successful" Americans); (2) the frame of reference called American culture is changing so fast, diversifying so greatly, that the prospects for such an adaptation may be improving (but it may be too late for the Menomini).

The Menomini are but a single case. The American culture, pluralistic and egalitarian in theory, appears to have functioned as a closed system for substantial parts of the population of the United States. It has ingested peoples with European and Anglo-Saxon cultural backgrounds, but it has rejected or blocked people with really divergent cultural or racial origins, unless, as in the case of the Japanese, there is a special kind of cultural convergence operating in crucial sectors, such as the achievement drive (DeVos 1968), and even for them, there have been complications.

This case study of Menomini adaptation is, therefore, relevant to a wider scene. Understanding the results of the confrontation between Menomini and Whiteman culture should help us to understand the results of some of the other confrontations that are occurring in our society in our time and between Western culture and other cultures.

The critical discongruities between cultural systems appear, in generalized terms, to be something like the following. In Western culture, and in United States middle class culture in particular, material power through use of technology is regarded as a means of accomplishing desired ends. In traditional Menomini culture material power cannot function by itself. Spiritual power is the basis for action and accomplishment. A man or woman without this spiritual power, or access to it, is powerless. In United States culture people must be aggressive in interpersonal relationships and social interaction to obtain personal recognition or business or professional success. In traditional Menomini culture aggressive people are suspected of being witches. In United States culture extraverted emotional expressiveness is valued as personal salesmanship. People should be friendly, evocative, lively. In Menomini culture emotions are rarely allowed to come to the surface. In United States culture the social interaction rate is fast, and matched by a torrent of words. In Menomini culture social interaction is slow and words are paced and few. In United States culture people are supposed to make decisions on the basis of rational and practical considerations. Among the traditional Menomini important decisions are made on the basis of dreams. There are other divergencies that will become apparent in this case study as the native-oriented group is described. We have cited these here in general terms in order to make one point clear—the differences between Western culture, particularly its United States version, and the traditional Menomini culture, could not easily be resolved. There are, of course, many regional, ethnic, and class differences in the non-Menomini population of the United States. The comparison is phrased in terms relevant to the Menomini-Whiteman confrontation as the Menomini appear to have experienced it.

The Consequences of Confrontation

When people are confronted with a politically and economically dominant cultural system[6] that is sharply divergent from their own and intolerant of divergence, they suffer severe disturbances in every sector of life. Their subsistence base may be destroyed, as was the case with most American Indian tribes. Their

---

[6] We will use the term "cultural system" to denote what is frequently encompassed by the terms "society" and "culture," following our usage, with Alan Beals, in *Culture in Process* (Beals, Spindler, and Spindler 1967). A cultural system is an organization of ideas, values, and norms for behavior, and of social interaction, statuses, roles, and authority. It includes ecological adaptation, technology, and actual groups. A cultural system has boundaries of some sort and the decision-making capacity. Although we think of "culture," in the strict definitional sense, as referring only to the ideational dimension of cultural systems, to avoid cumbersome usage and where meaning is apparent, we occasionally use "culture" to stand for cultural system.

political status is radically altered. The roles and statuses within the established cultural system are obliterated or seriously threatened. These external conditions are matched or exceeded by internal processes. The self-image is damaged, and the sense of identity that all functioning cultures provide is made ambiguous or is lost. Emotional controls, reinforced as they are in all communities by social sanctions, break down. The very process of thinking may become disorganized, for the logical and instrumental linkages that once seemed self-evident and valid are no longer so (G. Spindler 1968). Wise old men become irrelevant. Tribal lore becomes ridiculous. Values and beliefs lose their credibility. A cultural system is a total way of thinking, perceiving, feeling, acting, and justifying one's actions.

When divergent cultural systems meet under conditions of dominance and subordination, the people in the subordinate system do not simply disappear. They adapt. They try to re-create the social and cultural bases for identity and for the maintenance of emotional and cognitive controls. Some move to an identification with the dominant system, irrespective of its divergence. In so doing, they must forget whatever they once were. The forgetting usually takes the form of active suppression of the past, and active identification with the confronting culture. These individuals are most of the acculturated Menomini. A few people in this situation are able to handle the confrontation by segmentalizing action and thought. They live compartmentalized social and occupational lives, and think, when involved in different situations, in different frames of reference. There are a few acculturated Menomini who have adapted in this way.

Other individuals, for a variety of reasons, including differences in experience, emotional stability, and social alignments, are unable to identify with either the new culture or the old, and mill about in a no-man's-land—socially, emotionally, and intellectually. Group alignments, opinions, and behavior patterns shift and turn, as people try desperately to make some sense out of their situation. These are the Menomini transitionals.

Yet others adapt by attempting to synthesize potentially divergent aspects of the confronting cultures in the form of religious or social movements. Among the Menomini the Peyotists seem to do this with some success. The ritual and belief of the Native American Church, as practiced by the Menomini, are an interweaving of traditional Menomini, pan-Indian, and Christan elements. This synthesis provides a basis for a consistent world view and a recognizable identity.

There is still another style of adaptation. People may attempt to exclude certain of the most discongruent aspects of the divergent confronting culture and maintain as much as possible of the traditional culture. By reducing the amount of discongruent cultural demand and by reaffirming the validity of the traditional culture they provide for themselves a basis for identity, and for the maintenance of cognitive and emotional controls. This is the native-oriented group among the Menomini. (See G. Spindler, 1968 for further discussion of theory).

This framework puts into sharper focus the adaptive processes involved in the Menomini situation. It is important that we see each of the acculturative categories in the Menomini population as an adaptive strategy. The native-oriented group, for example, should not be understood simply as consisting of stubborn people who will not give up the past. Their way of life should be seen not as a sort of magical survival of disembodied traditional cultural elements but rather as the manner in which this group has tried to cope with the confrontation between the culture of their ancestors and Western culture, in the various forms in which it has been encountered by them.

Likewise, the Peyotists should not be seen as simply a group of deviants who are deviant for the sake of being deviant, or as a group of neurotics, or as a group of "natives" who have been "turned on" and who are stretching their minds with the bud of the cactus *Lophophera williamsii*. They are a group of people who are trying desperately to get along in a semantic environment that is so deeply conflicted that there is no way to make sense out of it. Peyotism provides them with a kind of ready-made solution. It puts together what everyone else has left apart.

The acculturated should not be seen simply as a group of exceptionally intelligent and hard-working Indians who have seen how good it is to be White middle or working class. They (or their parents and grandparents) have coped with the confrontation of discongruent cultures by becoming culturally and psychologically White, even though they have retained a generalized Indian social identity. They should neither be criticized nor praised for their adaptation. It meets with the approval of White authority figures, particularly priests, teachers, and government officials, but it is just another strategy of adaptation.

There are other types of adaptation that are not represented in strength among the Menomini. Neither Peyotism or nativistic reaffirmation are transformative, revolutionary, or militant. They are accommodative. The acculturated personnel are more change-oriented but basically they, too, "get along" with the conditions of existence as they are.

Transformative or alterative movements of a militant character have only begun to become significant among the Menomini. Red, or Indian Power, a militant identity-asserting movement, has some adherents. If such a movement comes in force it will be attractive to transitional and acculturated elements who feel most acutely a threat of personal deprivation in recent events.

That Which Was Lost

What is the culture that the Menomini have lost? The next chapter will deal with some aspects of it as the present way of life of the native-oriented group is described, and connections made to the traditional culture, but no single chapter, or single volume, however massive, could really do justice to this lost culture. Everyone who has done research with the Menomini, including such people as Leonard Bloomfield, Felix and Marie Keesing, J. S. Slotkin, Sister Inez Hilger, Francis Densmore, W. G. Hoffman, Samuel Barrett, and Alanson Skinner, has recognized explicitly the richness, subtlety, and complexity of traditional Menomini culture.[7] We have ourselves seen enough, even in the attenuated versions of this culture still operant in the native-oriented group (and among the Peyotists in a different context) to come to some understanding of this com-

---

[7] This list does not include people like David Ames, Gary Olfield, Rachael Sady, Robert Edgerton, and others, who have done significant, recent work with the Menomini but who did not study the traditional culture.

plexity. However, to gain more depth one has to go back to the writings (such as Hoffman 1896, Skinner 1913, 1915, and Skinner and Satterlee 1915) done before the flu epidemic of 1917–1918, which took most of the elders and thereby dealt the prospects of much continuity in Menomini tradition a severe blow.

The Menomini had a complex cosmogony. They thought of the universe as divided into strata (including the earth as one), with deities and powers resident in each that had different power relationships with each other and with man. The underground strata, in opposition to those strata above the earth, were the evil underworld, where the White Bear, the Underground Panther, the White Deer, and the Horned Snake dwelt. These forces were inimical to man.[8] The residents of the upper strata, in contrast, were friendly to man, or at least could be placated by him. The Thunderers, in the level just below Me·c-awe·tok, the supreme force in the universe, were especially friendly to man, and waged unceasing war against the horned serpents, who were man's most consistent persecutors.

There were innumerable lesser gods, genii, and goblins, such as the Flying Skeleton, the Wanderer, the Little God Boys, the Cannibal Spirits, and the North Giant, and there was a system of complex sacred bundles. Each bundle contained "medicines," such as "thunder eggs" (rounded stones), miniature war and lacrosse clubs, roots, powders, and so forth, which were invested with powers evoked by ritual, song, and reverence, and which could do great good or harm. There were also pictographs, done on birchbark or hides (see Fig. 2). These were often used as wrappings for bundles, and functioned as memory joggers (mnemonic devices) for the owner of the bundle as the complex rituals necessary for their use were carried out. Others were used in the same way by storytellers. Figure 2 shows an unusually complex scroll, made of birchbark, exhibited by one old man as he told the tales. He inherited it from his father, and it could be traced to his father's grandfather, but no further back (Skinner 1913:74–78). Each strip can be "read" in some detail. The bottom strip, for example, shows, from right to left, the village of the Thunderers in the sky, then Wickano, the leader of the Thunderers, the powerful wind which he controls and his clouds, Wickano at his resting place, one of his associates, and the rain which belongs to them, Wickano again, a tornado, the clouds behind which Thunderers stalk their prey, and, last (far left), a Thunderer pouncing upon one of the evil serpents from the underworld. Certain songs go with different parts of the scroll and punctuate the storytelling.[9]

There were many dance and ritual associations, including the Tobacco, Braves, Harvest, Totem Animals, Rain, and South Wind Dances and the Bear, Buffalo, Thunder, and Witch associations. Each association or dance group had its own songs, employed certain medicines, and controlled certain powers. There were also several classes of shamans, some of whom combatted witches, others

[8] This statement must be modified in respect to certain deities and forces. The White Bear, for example, holds up the earth and is the sacred ancestor of the Menomini.

[9] Such scrolls were more common among the Chippewa, with whom they may have originated, but irrespective of origin, they were a significant part of Menomini culture when it was studied by Hoffman and by Skinner.

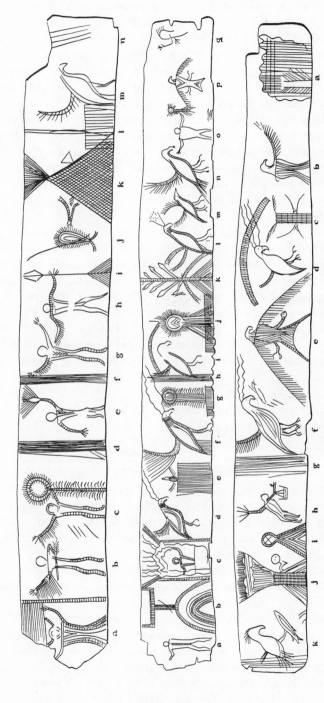

Figure 2. Three birchbark strips containing records of Thunderbirds. (From Skinner 1913:76.)

of whom witched (in many cases these two activities were combined), some of whom were clairvoyant, some of whom were concerned with all forms of curing disease, and some of whom had special skills, such as jugglery.

The folklore of the Menomini is complex. Skinner (Skinner and Satterlee 1915) collected 129 episodes, but he acknowledges the existence of many more that he or his assistant, John Satterlee, did not record. There are sacred tales of the origin of the universe, tales of the culture hero *Mɛʔnapos*, fairy tales, true stories, and tales of European origin modified to Menomini taste. There are themes of power loss and gain, soul loss, vengeance, love, consequences of bad behavior, dreaming, imposters, contests, and many others. There are props, such as the magic canoe that goes by itself, the inexhaustible kettle that never gets empty, the mummified dog kept in a box, ever ready to come to life when needed, the singing snowshoes that precede the hunter to the lodge and sing like birds, an animal (lynx) head ball that, when batted or thrown at any object, bites it and brings it back. These and many other props enliven the stories as they were told by old men and women nearly every evening during the winter.

The traditional culture mapped the universe for the Menomini individual. It provided a style of thinking and imaginative content. It also provided instrumentalities for survival, some of them material, such as weapons, tools, means of transportation; some of them intangible (from the Western point of view), such as "power" to be acquired through dream and vision and maintained by ritual. It provided a language that was subtle, complex, and radically different from any Western language in its organization of action and object, time and occurrence. It provided a social map within which all persons could be placed, with kin terms and associated appropriate behaviors, and totem and clan identifications. It explained origins, geography, marriage, conception, birth, life crises, and death. It provided a philosophy of education, rules for teachers, a theory of man in nature, a set of values to live and die by.

The Plan

Menomini culture, in its total complexity and subtlety, has been lost. There was no place for it in the scheme of things that resulted from the Whiteman's occupation of the New World as the Whiteman defined this scheme. The Menomini culture as a way of thinking as well as a way of doing was discongruent with Western culture, and no form of real divergence was tolerated in the Whiteman American mania for assimilation and conformity. It is tragic that this was so. However, this book is not about this tragedy. It is about the ways in which the people called Menomini have coped with the conditions they encountered. Therefore, because it is about Menomini, more space is given to those who have kept their culture in some form—the native-oriented group and the Peyotists. Because the story would be incomplete without them, we include, in Chapter 4, an analysis of the transitionals and, in Chapter 5, some consideration of the acculturated adaptation. The book is unbalanced as a representation of contemporary reality, for the transitional and acculturated individuals far out-

The authors lived in a tent near the northeast edge of Menomini lands during most of their fieldwork. This brought them into close proximity to the native-oriented and Peyote groups, which lived not far away.

number the native-oriented people and Peyotists combined, and neither of these latter adaptations will be decisive in the future. However, to evaluate the significance of the various adaptive strategies in accordance with the number of people involved in a given adaptation or even their future role would be quite wrong for our purposes. We are concerned with the broader implications of the Menomini as one case. The focus is upon those segments of the population that have adapted by exclusion, reaffirmation, and synthesis. The next chapter is about the native-oriented group, and Chapter 3 is about the Peyotists.

There is another problem of content selection. We started our fieldwork with the Menomini in 1948. We worked all summer long, each summer, through 1954, with the exception of one season (1951). We have visited the Menomini almost every year since then, did some intensive fieldwork in 1961, and in 1969, and we maintained contacts and friendships with some persons in each major sociocultural category. Our fieldwork procedures are discussed in detail in another publication (G. Spindler and L. Spindler 1970), so we will not describe them in this case study. Which Menomini should we describe? The Menomini of 1947–1948? The Menomini of 1954? Of 1960? Or of 1969–1970? There are several considerations involved. Some anthropologists use the "ethnographic present" in describing extinct cultural systems. We could write a description of traditional Menomini culture, using the present tense, based upon what we could reconstruct of the old culture from our field notes, and the reports of Hoffman, Skinner, and others, who visited the Menomini before their culture was broken. For some purposes this would be useful, but not for our purposes, for we are primarily concerned with adaptation, and especially with the acute phases of recent adaptation. We are left, then, with the periods of our own direct experience, given time depth via the observations of others. We have elected to describe the situation as it existed more or less consistently in the decade between 1951 and 1961,[10] when termination of the reservation status, and federal jurisdiction, occurred. At that time the former Menomini reservation became Menominee County, and Menominee Enterprises, Inc., became management. The process of change was accelerated with termination. The disappearance of the last vestiges of the Menomini culture was hastened. The diffusion of the Menomini identity was reinforced. The people are still struggling to make a living, to get an education, to gain self-respect. They are Menomini in the loose sense that they are at least in part genetically Menomini, and in the very loose sense of affiliation with others called Menomini. Most are not culturally Menomini. The acculturative adaptations we have already described still exist, however. The native-oriented group still holds ni·mihε·twan ceremonies.[11] The metε·wen has not been held on Menomini land since termination, but members of the lodge travel to nearby sites where it is still given. Peyote activity in Menominee County has slackened, but members still participate in meetings nearby. The adaptive strategies described for these two groups are less apparent among the Menomini, however, than they were just before termination. Nevertheless, we choose to concentrate on these groups and their strategies, for it is here that we can see most clearly the confrontation and its consequences.

*　　*　　*　　*

About our father the God Above, whom all worship, and none have seen: this song is in his praise, this true one. This is the way the words were given to the old lady who dreamed our drum. The Creator promised to help the whole world through the drum. The gods below helped also. Never shall this earth be destroyed, upset, or turned wrong.[12]

The song:

> *God himself has agreed to help this earth.*
> *The earth shall never be destroyed.*
> *The earth shall be protected by us.*
> *The world shall never be destroyed.*

*　　*　　*　　*

This first chapter provides the framework for the whole book. The next chapter is about the native-oriented group and its culture in the light of its past. Though the present way of life of this group is an adaptation to con-

---

[10] We will therefore be using a short-term "ethnographic present." Except in Chapter 6, or unless otherwise specified, all statements and data apply to the period before termination.

[11] We attended a major seasonal rite, in which several new members were installed, in August 1965. Several of the members are attending a major ceremony, on the date we write this (November 8, 1969), at a site near Menominee County.

[12] Thomas Hog, as told to Skinner (1915:201).

temporary conditions, it is also a product of the history of the Menomini, and of the traditional culture. To provide time depth for the picture of current adaptation we have, therefore, drawn from ethnohistoric sources, from the writings of observers who met the Menomini before the old way of life was reduced, as well as from our own observations and those of contemporary ethnographers.

2

Omɛ·ʔnomɛ·neʾw[1]

What Are They Like?

THE FOLLOWING EXAMPLES of cultural and psychological characteristics are
drawn from observations of the contemporary native-oriented group and from
older sources describing the Menomini of the past. The latter are printed in
italics so the reader can more easily compare the two kinds of statements.

Our friend did not seem quite as relaxed as we rembered her to be. Then
the child on the bed began to cry restlessly. She got up slowly and walked
hesitatingly to the bed to stroke her daughter's head. Then turned to us almost
apologetically to say, "She's got some kind of illness. She's hot, and she hasn't
kept anything down for two days." We did what we could—gave the child
a little aspirin—and offered to take her in to the hospital to see the doctor.
Then it dawned on us that last year there had been no baby and that the
one swaddled in blankets looked virtually new-born. "Yes. She's new. She came
three days ago." Then the story came out. . . .
Our friend's husband had gone on one of his long trips to a neighboring
reservation many miles away. In the meantime our friend had borne her fourth
child during his absence and while everyone else was gone. She was isolated.
She had no car and could not walk to the highway to get help. Her five year
old daughter had become ill. There was no food left in the house. She said
all of this quietly, with none of the hysteria or blaming that would have been
normal for a woman in similar circumstances in our world. She merely stated
the facts. [Reported in G. Spindler 1963:359]

*Whatever misfortune may befall them they never allow themselves to lose
their calm composure of mind, in which they think that happiness especially*

---

[1] We use the native term for wild-rice people, from which the word "Menomini" is
derived, to indicate that this chapter is about the people who have tried to keep their
culture, even though they only rarely now actually harvest the wild rice that was an important
staple of their ancestors.

A member of the Medicine Lodge and Dream Dance standing before his house in 1952. Today he is the most active leader of this group, but he lives in town.

consists. . . . Even the pangs of childbirth, although most bitter, are so concealed or conquered by the women that they do not even groan. [Father Jouvency, 1710, in *Jesuit Relations* 1896 vol. 1:277]

After a year's absence, during which we thought often about our Menomini friends and with great anticipation about our return in the spring, we drove up to an area near the Zoar community hall where the Dream Dance rituals were held, where many members of the native-oriented group lived. There we saw a group standing and sitting about. Some of the men were playing poker on a blanket spread on the ground. Others were kibitzing. We parked our car, got out, and tried to walk casually, not run, into the circle of what we perceived as old friends who would greet us with the enthusiasm of long-lost members of the family. But we had forgotten what the native-oriented Menomini were like! Expressionless faces greeted us. Some even turned away, as though preoccupied with other matters more interesting. Only the children stared, but quietly. I walked over to the group of people clustered around the poker game and joined the kibitzers. Ranks opened so I had a place to stand and a clear view of the game, but otherwise no special notice was taken of my arrival. I stood across from a man about my age with whom I had, I felt, formed an especially close friendship, and who had been enormously helpful to me in my research in the past. He continued with his game, taking no notice of me whatsoever. I began to feel acutely uncomfortable. Perhaps there had been a long winter of gossip about the White strangers who had

Our friends are grouped around a blanket spread on the ground, playing poker. The shelters were built for and occupied during the annual fair and pageant.

invaded their privacy for too long. Perhaps we were suspect of witchcraft, or at least of bringing bad luck. Finally, after several minutes of paranoid fantasy on my part, my friend Nepenahkwat glanced up, smiled quietly, and said calmly, "Hello George, I see you made it." And then continued with his game.

We stayed for several hours that afternoon. During the first hours we gradually became aware of the fact that the people were glad to see us, that they had thought about us during our absence, and that they had looked forward to our return. We also reestablished our timing and role-taking in social interaction with native-oriented Menomini. We realized again that these were different people, with a different psychology, and a different set of norms for proper behavior. Overt emotionality is not displayed. The loud, overstated greeting normal for the situation in our own society would not only have been in very bad taste according to Menomini standards, but it would have been virtually impossible for a native-oriented Menomini adult, properly educated and formed in the traditional framework, to act that way even if he had, conceivably, wanted to. [G. Spindler 1963:357–358]

. . . they have a mild but independent expression of countenance. . . . [Major Pike, 1810, cited in Hoffman 1896:34]

. . . My grandfather remarked, that he regarded the Menomonees as the most peaceful, brave, and faithful of all the tribes who ever served under him [Mr. Grignon, 1856, cited in Hoffman 1896:34]

It is not because it is me. It is not because I know these things that I speak this way. I am not proud just because I know this little. It is because my father was important in this and I got it from him, not because of myself. But it is because my father was there when they brought the drum to my grandfather's place. [Menomini elder, addressing the Dream Dance group]

A few "true stories" are told for the purpose of inculcating the principles of honor, virtue, and bravery among the children. Many of these have a moral, either stated or implied, contrary to the popular idea of North American folklore. The four most common of these are chastity, bravery, reverence, and guarding against undue pride. [Skinner 1915:235].

Sit quiet like a stone, and let thoughts come to you. Think about a leaf in a pool. [Menomini elder, speaking to his grandson]

. . . They [witches] done that to my father. He used to be one of the leaders of the Medicine Drum. He owned a drum. The one P. has. Well, my father's eyes pretty near killed him in those days. One old fellow used to stay a lot here and knew the persons who done that to him. It made his eye white and he just had one eye after that. [Did he know who did this?] *Yes, he knew who did it, but didn't want the fellow to know that he knew it was him.* [Menomini woman, in L. Spindler, field notes]

Witches and wizards are persons supposed to possess the agency of familiar spirits, from whom they receive power to inflict diseases on their enemies, prevent the good luck of the hunter, and the success of the warrior. They are believed to fly invisibly at pleasure from place to place; to turn themselves into bears, wolves, foxes, owls, bats, and snakes. [Reverend Peter Jones 1843:145, cited in Hoffman 1896:152]

I feel that sometimes a baby being born, maybe one of our grandfathers might have his spirit in the little boy. There's one funny thing about the little boy I lost. Old men used to understand babies. Now, nobody understands their language. That baby used to talk all the time. We gave him an Indian name but he wasn't satisfied with it. He had some little power, maybe from his grandfather. My brother-in-law was married to a White girl and I never told her about eating when she was that way. She had a habit of feeding my baby and you know, you're not supposed to kiss a baby or anything then, and have to keep soiled things away from men's clothes and always keep clean. I never had any soiled things laying around. Nowadays it's easy with those pads. Now, my aunt says she wishes things had been like that when she was young. Well, she fed my baby and a few days after the baby had stomach trouble and diarrhea. *I wasn't really blaming her.* I was thinking the little boy had some power that was killed by her. And this boy [she points to her son] here seems to know ahead when I'm going to menstruate. He wets the bed each time. My aunt says I got to be careful of him, as someone must have ate with him when she was menstruating. [Menomini woman, in L. Spindler 1962:40–41]

There is no Nation among 'em which has not a sort of Juglers or Conjuerers, which some look upon to be Wizzards, but in my Opinion there is no Great reason to believe 'em such, or to think that their Practice favours any thing of a Communication with the Devil. These Impostors came them-

selves to be reverenced as Prophets which fore-tell Futurity. They will needs be look'd upon to have an unlimited Power. They boast of being able to make it Wet or Dry; to cause a Calm or a Storm; to render Land Fruitful or Barren; and, in a word, to make Hunters Fortunate or Unfortunate. They also pretend to Physick, and to apply Medicine, but which are such, for the most part as having little Virtue at all in 'em, especially to Cure that Distemper which they pretend to. [Hennepin 1689:50, cited in Hoffman 1896:141]

. . . The oldest leader of the Dream Dance group (and the most powerful) took liberties with a sacred drum left in the charge of a younger man and made a public apology for the action in a speech. He said:

My children, I am good to you. I care for you all the time. I pray for you to the Gentle Spirit. I cure you when you get sick, with good medicines. Somebody here does not feel good about things somehow. Now, all right . . . I did not take that drum away from anybody. I did not want to hurt anyone's feelings. . . . That is all I have to say. [G. Spindler, field notes]

The harmony which subsists among the savages is in truth displayed not only by their words, but in actual conduct. The chiefs who are the most influential and well-to-do are on equal footing with the poorest, and even the boys—with whom they converse as they do with persons of discretion. They warmly support and take in hand the cause of one another among friends; and when there are any disputes they proceed therein with great moderation. . . . Seldom are there quarrels among them. [From the memoirs of Nicholas Perrote, 1667, quoted in Keesing 1939:40]

Yes. Some go to both [the *mete·wen* or Dream Dance and the Peyote church]. But it isn't good. *But we don't like to tell them not to come to the meetings.* The old men all think it keeps our prayers from gettin' to our grandfather's spirits. Lots of times when something goes wrong with our prayers, they think those ones who go to both bring in evil and keep prayers from gettin' there. [Menomini woman, in L. Spindler, field notes]

I have had no trouble with the savages. None of them have been angry with me because I declared the false divinity of the sun, of the thunder, the bear, of the underground panther, of Manabus, of their dreams, nor because I spoke against superstitious feasts and against the Jugglers {Cese·ko}. They had no objection to cover themselves before me . . . there were some who fasted without blackening their faces. . . . [Father André, 1671–1689, in *Jesuit Relations 1896–1901*, vol. lvii:265–282]

No one has the right, on the basis of position or prestige, to exercise direct authority over another, not even a father over his son. Children are given their earnings from the dances put on for tourists to spend as they will. A child of five years may own and keep the money thus gained. There is love and honor in traditional Menomini marriage, but no "obeying." Strong men do not order weak ones about. [G. Spindler 1963:376]

The savage does not know what it is to obey. . . . The father does not venture to exercise authority over his son, nor does the chief dare to give commands to his soldier. . . . If the chiefs possess some influence over their men . . . it is only through the liberal presents and feasts which they give. [Nicholas Perrote, first French fur trader to visit the Menomini in 1667, in Blair 1911:144–145]

Among themselves, the rights of the individuals were paramount. A husband might not sell or dispose of his wife's or children's property, nor had any other person, except the owner, any right to them. If a member of the family chose to bargain off personal possessions, no other member ever interfered in any way. Even infants had the sole right to what was theirs. [Skinner 1913:6]

One dream I always think about. Just before this baby was born I used to have a garden where this building is. I dreamt I was out there picking corn. J. B. came over and wanted me to help him right away pick potatoes. I kind of laughed in the dream about J. B. because he never had a garden. I told him I'd help him. I had to get my corn in right away that evening. He told me if I helped him he'd give me half of his potatoes. I saw potatoes ready to be dug up late in the Fall. I saw J. B. startin' on one row with sacks here and there. Then he was gone and I was alone. While I was bending down it seemed like there was a light above me gettin' brighter and brighter. I was afraid to look up. I was alone. It looked like some kind of sun. I saw *Se·sos'* [Jesus'] face. I got scairt and couldn't look longer. I tried to find a place to hide. I was all alone and couldn't find a place to hide. He was all white. I told my aunt about that dream and she told me maybe I was goin' to be left alone. She said it was a good dream and the Lord was watchin' over me. I said I felt like I was alone. She almost guessed my dream. I was left alone September, October, December. W. left for awhile and lived with M.'s wife at Eagle River. After the baby was born, he came back Christmas. He asked if he could come home. While he was gone, J. B. used to come and cut wood and bring water for no pay—just meals. [Menomini woman, in L. Spindler, field notes]

For a girl to dream of things on high meant long life, happiness, virtue, and perhaps social elevation. In one instance a girl dreamt of a large fat man, who appeared and told her that she would have a long life, that she had power over the winds, and that she might hear what people said of her, no matter how far away they were when they spoke. She dreamt also of the sun, who said she would have a long life and promised protection. Should she desire anything and pray to the sun for it, it would be granted her. The sun commanded her always to wear a red waist as a sign of the eight virgins who lived in the east. They too would hear her prayers. All these things were a reward for her suffering, for she had fasted ten days. [Skinner 1913:43]

At a tribal council meeting held to discuss the budget for the following year, a great deal of criticism was directed at the large expenditure for installation of a heavy cable suspended across the mill pond, from which logs were snagged and pulled over to a lift. During the heat of the arguing, old Kime·wan rose and addressed the mixed group of conservative, transitional, and elite members in Menomini, saying:

There has been much talk about the money that has been spent. Many people seem unhappy. I do not know much about these things, but I see what is going on. Now let it be said that I do not understand the purpose that our brothers had in installing that cable. But I have noticed that it has some use. This fall, as the leaves began to drop from the trees, the birds were all lined up on it, wing to wing. For them it is a good thing, because it gives them all an even start on the way south. [G. Spindler, field notes]

We came to a cottage of an ancient witty man, that had a great familie and many children, his wife old, nevertheless handsome. They were of a nation called Malhonmines; that is the nation of Oats. [Radisson, 1654, cited in Kessing 1939:42]

One day a forest fire started here. I picked up W. in my truck to go out to it with me. On the way W. said, "It's too bad we didn't stop to get Fred [his brother-in-law] because he could tell us exactly where the fire was. [But he said that Fred was asleep.] It took about one-hundred men workin' hard to put that fire out." Then, on the way back, W. said it was really too bad that we didn't pick up Fred and take him with us, because, "He's got a nice extinguisher about this long [6 inches] and all he would have to do is wobble it about a little and the whole fire would have been put out without all that expense and trouble."
"There's a lot of kiddin' goin' around here about your brother-in-law. The one 'brags him up.' the other 'runs him down.'" [Menomini male, in G. Spindler field notes]

In 1911, while attending an outdoor ceremony of the dreamers, I stopped to talk with John Keshena, an Indian storekeeper, when chief Sabatis came up. Sabatis at once began to revile Keshena, warning me to purchase nothing of him. "Tobacco, anywhere else five cents, ten cents he charges! He lies, he steals, he cheats!"

During this tirade Keshena grinned pleasantly, and seemed not in the least offended. At the conclusion of his outburst chief Sabatis turned to me and said, smiling at my surprise, "Oh that is just our Indian way! I can joke with him, he is my brother-in-law!" [Skinner 1913:20]

INTERPRETATION

The Menomini in the native-oriented group think, say, and do all of these things. These samples of behaviors and attitudes furnish important clues for understanding what present-day Menomini are like. Except for the historical materials (indicated in italics), these are excerpts from conversations with and observations of Menomini in the present native-oriented group. This homogeneous group includes only about 3 percent of the Menomini population, yet it represents traditional Menomini culture as it exists today in its attenuated but most visible form.[2] The Medicine Lodge ceremony and the Dream Dance are still alive among the native-oriented group; members believe in the importance of power and the guardian spirit; menstrual taboos are observed by many of the women; belief in the power of witchcraft flourishes; the members still utilize hunting, fishing, and gathering subsistence techniques and use the Menomini language in ceremonies (some elders speak almost no English).

Members of the native-oriented group share a patterned set of values, attitudes, and perceptions about the natural world and the world of people around them. One part of this shared pattern, expressed in the examples of behaviors, includes emotional control. The Menomini woman who bore a child while alone and cared for another sick child at the same time seemed to exhibit control under the most trying of situations. Her control, however, is different from that of most White women in our society. The fear and hysteria were absent, as she had learned to live with isolation and had learned to "accept" misery when present. Isolation in the woods during menstruation was a familiar situation. She was not "controlling" the fear and anxiety. They were not there. She displayed a quality that might be called *equanimity under duress*. She also displayed a dependent, waiting attitude toward fate and what it might bring. She had made a sacrifice of food and tobacco to the Dream Dance drum for which she was the keeper, and that rested in its coverings on a special bench on the eastern side of her kitchen, where the light of the new day would touch it each morning through the nearby window. So she had reason to hope that the spirits might take notice of her predicament and take pity on her. Apparently, it worked, as it had many times in the past, from her point of view, since we arrived and took action.

This characteristic attitude or quality of waiting expectantly may be termed "latescent" (L. Spindler 1962). These attitudes are related to power. Although most of the members of the native-oriented group did not receive a guardian spirit through a vision while fasting, having power is all important today for survival; and, as is seen in the samples of behavior, dreams are still used to predict the future. Power is secured by displaying passivity while fasting and dreaming, quiescence (lack of excessive bodily motion, silence), receptivity, and expectancy. These attitudes can be subsumed under the term "latescent" (activity existing in possibility, depending upon an outside entity for realization). This term char-

---

[2] The language spoken (other than English) is most often Menomini. The Medicine Lodge and Dream Dance, shared with other woodland tribes, has certain characteristic Menomini features, and the cosmology and mythology is identifiably Menomini. However, a synthesis with southern Chippewa, Potowatomi, and Ottawa has been taking place for generations. These central Algonkian peoples were much alike, culturally, when contact first occurred. They probably became more alike as time went on, but particularly so after reservations were formed and the viability of the traditional cultures was seriously threatened. As a response to the overwhelming pressure of the White cultural system, the conservative elements of the tribes drew together. Cultural synthesis as well as genetic fusion occurred. This does not invalidate the description of this group as native oriented, since it is, or of labeling it "Menomini," since its members are on the tribal roll (with a few exceptions).

acterizes the affective tone of social interaction among and the shared personality characteristics of native-oriented Menomini.

This attitude of passive acceptance and receptivity is constantly evidenced in behaviors and beliefs. For example, in the quotation concerning the father who was witched and losing his eyesight (p. 21), the Menomini woman stated in a matter of fact tone, "Yes, he knew who done it, but didn't want the fellow to know that he knew it was him." When women retired to the menstrual house to be separated from men, as they were a threat to a man's power at this period, it was stressed that, as one informant said, "They had to be quiet." When parents selected a husband for their daughter, he was unquestioningly accepted by her. When a strange man came to marry her, a Menomini lady merely commented to the authors, in restrospect, "I was surprised." Her voice implied, however, that she was also frightened and did not want to marry the man. This seemingly passive approach to life does not mean despondency, as the native-oriented Menomini are resilient, vital, and flexible in their adjustment to daily problems—the air of expectancy and the potential for action are always present.

The quality of equanimity under duress is closely related to these latescent attitudes. The passive, quiescent, waiting expectancy is an important part of the Menomini ability to endure privation and hardship, but latescence is based on the expectancy that if the proper rituals are performed, the fates will provide— unless the fates decide otherwise—while equanimity under duress is part of a survival drive, which takes into account the realities of the situation and makes it possible to retain the necessary emotional balance even when the reality conditions are very threatening.

The marked control of expressive emotionality, apparent in the description of the reception of the authors by the native-oriented group after a long absence (p. 19), is congruent with the other qualities just described. It is more readily observable and of a somewhat different order, yet is another facet of the same behavioral pattern. We found that the members of the group were actually glad to see us, had thought about us during our absence, and had looked forward to our return. A loud, expressive greeting to anyone would be completely at odds with the native-oriented Menomini pattern for interaction, either with people or in their environment. The necessity for composure and equanimity when confronted with any strong emotion is an accepted part of their action system. Loud voices are threatening and disturbing. A group of twenty native-oriented Menomini can sit in a small room carrying on conversations without the noise level ever reaching the point at which one has difficulty hearing his friend, and there are long silences that no one attempts to fill with talk. Silence is not embarrassing. People, even children, are never ordered about. Even pointing a finger at someone is considered in poor taste—one points with one's lips. Asking direct questions of anyone is distasteful. The Menomini language itself contains a preponderance of goal-action, or passive-type, construction rather than the actor-action or command-type construction used extensively in English. Direct criticism of others is not expressed, either in their presence or behind their backs. One might say to another person about someone else, "There could be some people here that don't do just right. Sometimes they could have enough to get along on but they try to get it from someone else."

This reduction of overt emotional response, especially aggressive response, is related to the importance of possessing power and the fear of power loss through witchcraft. If a person controls expression of aggression of any form—by refraining from gossip, practicing generosity, hospitality, tolerance—he will not be a target for an act of witchcraft. Any old person may be a witch. A native-oriented Menomini cannot really blame another person for committing a "sin," even though he is himself directly involved. This is apparent from the description of behavior dealing with the White girl (p. 21) who had fed a baby while menstruating, causing its death, according to its mother, who merely said, "I wasn't really blaming her. I was thinking the little boy had some power that was killed by her." There can be no personalized guilt feelings about deviant behaviors since a person's strength or weaknesses are dependent upon the amount of power she or he has at the time.

Another shared value is autonomy. Each person is responsible for his own behavior, and no one has the right to exercise authority over another or his possessions. "Even infants had sole right to what was theirs," Skinner remarked (1913:6). No one is his neighbor's keeper. When a ceremonial gathering is to be announced, a skapɛ·wes (messenger) is appointed. He travels about from house to house, passing tobacco to those who should be notified, and telling them the time and place. However, the tobacco is not given only to the "head" of the household or family. It is passed to every person who might be expected to come, to man and wife, brother and sister, and each older child. Collective notifications are never given; even when people from another tribe are to be notified, it is necessary to travel to the places where they live and pass tobacco to each individual. The same principle applies to transportation. People are expected to arrange their own. Even old people may not be taken care of in this regard, and an old man of eighty, who is important to the conduct of the ceremonial because he is the only one who knows the ritual, will have to stumble across the fields and through the dark woods to the gathering by himself, unless a member of his household happens to be coming to the gathering and the old man is standing by the car when it is started up. This is not individuality, as we conceive of it. Whites often call the Menomini "individualistic." Their latescent attitude and seeming reluctance to originate social interaction give support to this stereotype held by the Whites. Autonomy should not be interpreted as not conforming to the norms of the group, as members of the native-oriented group conform closely. In fact, part of the conformity is to be autonomous. However, no one is anyone else's "boss." No one is responsible for anyone else's welfare, except in those areas of reciprocation dictated by kinship obligations. No one can be discredited because of the actions of another, not even a father by his own son. The attitude of acceptance of others' behaviors is a part of this complex. Examples of acceptance of religious differences, given previously (p. 22), are to the point.

Another quality, more peripheral in nature yet a part of the shared pattern for behavior, is a keen sense of humor. This is constantly apparent in day-to-day interaction. The example given from the speech of the important elder, Kime·wan, is typical (p. 24). The comment about the controversial cable serving as a prop for the birds disrupted the council meeting and gave the budgeteers something to think about. Humor among the native-oriented Menomini may serve as a release of tensions built up by the constraints imposed upon expressiveness and particularly the expression of aggression. This is apparent in the relations between a man and his father-in-law and brother-in-law. The examples of behaviors presented previously include some of the ribald and grotesquely humorous remarks passed between brothers-in-law and by one about the other—"The one 'brags him up,' the other 'runs him down'" (p. 24).

Another related quality which belongs to the ideal of striving for harmony in interpersonal relations referred to by all students of Menomini culture is hospitality. In the past "it was considered a duty to look out for a guest's welfare and to treat him with the utmost respect" (Skinner 1913:6). All strangers, unless hostile, were to be considered as guests. The cautious regard for the wishes of others was revealed in the patterned treatment of the host. He addressed the guests in the set words: "N'hau! Come in if you so desire, but you need not if you do not wish to." When the food was brought by his wife, he would say, "Now eat, if you so desire, but refrain, if you do not care for this kind of food. It is what we eat every day; we have nothing better to offer you" (Skinner 1913:6).

The shared qualities of the native-oriented group form a pattern—equanimity under duress, latescence, control of overt emotionality and aggression, autonomy, keen sense of humor, and hospitality. The reader might well ask from what kinds of materials this pattern was derived. The authors observed and interacted with the members of this small group over a period of years. Observations of the kinds of behaviors that have been described were carefully recorded. The activities of individuals in the group as they acted in a wide variety of situations over a long period of time could be observed. This "participant-observer" technique is the hallmark of anthropological fieldwork, and there is no substitute for it. Other techniques were also used in collecting data (See G. Spindler and L. Spindler 1970, Chapter 11, for a detailed description of how fieldwork was done among the Menomini).

The Rorschach Projective Technique (the "inkblot" test) was given to seventeen adult males and eight adult females in the native-oriented group, and life histories were collected from two of the males and four of the females. There are many problems concerning the validity of interpretations for the Rorschach, even in our own society, and the problems are compounded by cross-cultural usage. In this particular application, however, the Rorschach seemed to produce results that were congruent with the other observations. Following is a brief interpretive summary of the Rorschach responses of the native-oriented Menomini (for details see G. Spindler 1955 and L. Spindler 1962).

Members of this group produce an adequate number of responses by usual standards, but there is a marked tendency for the range of content to be narrow and for various stimulus properties of the inkblots to be used very selectively. The perceptual field can therefore be described as narrow. The responses that are given within this narrow field cannot, however, be described as "rigid," as one would expect them to be if respondents from our own society were thus "constricted." That which is used is used flexibly. Overt emotionality is not displayed. (This is a very consistent feature.) Responses are careful, and obvious features of the blots, such as bright color, are rarely used. More subtle features, such as achromatic shading, are emphasized. The action quality of human figures in movement is passive. Human figures are rarely projected as doing anything but "sitting," "standing," or "facing that way." Motives for human action are not imputed. Animal figures are most frequently projected as being in action, such as "eating," or "climbing a tree," or "sneaking away through the brush," or "looking out from behind a tree." They are rarely perceived as engaged in aggressive action, such as attacking another animal. The concentration on animal figures is such that the perceptual structure could be described as zoomorphic. There is little content that we could describe as "morbid." The passivity and the quiescent quality of responses is not hopeless or depressive. The intellectual functions are adequate—there are virtually no distortions or breaks in reality. There is little drive to produce more than is necessary to complete the task as perceived. No native-oriented respondent asked, "How many responses do most people give?" as many acculturated respondents did. Once a response is given, it is regarded as a problem solved, and there is little point in solving it again for the sake of accumulating a "good score."

In summary, the typical native-oriented pattern of psychological characteristics revealed in Rorschach responses appears to be highly introverted, sensitive to the environment but able to maintain equilibrium despite its variations, not achievement oriented, lacking generally in overt emotional responsiveness and exhibiting a high degree of rational control over it when it does appear, motivated more by biologically oriented drives than by self-projective fantasy, intellectually uncomplicated but reality based and adequate in terms of its setting, lacking in rigidity, without evidence of high anxiety, tension, or internal conflict. This picture of the native-oriented Menomini suggests that the basic premises upon which the personality is predicated are radically different than the ones we understand in Western culture. It is limited without being constricted, sensitive without being imputative. It is a type that accepts fate, retains equanimity under duress, and achieves control under provocation. However, it is unsuited for the competitive struggle in a society that is structured around social and economic manipulation and requires focused interpersonal aggression for achievement within its framework.[3]

It is apparent that the patterns of psychological characteristics derived from analysis of Rorschach responses is congruent with the shared cultural patterns derived from analysis of behavior in the environment. The inward-oriented, cautious approach to the outside world revealed by the Rorschach seems related to the dependent type of value orientations, the deep fear of witchcraft, and the latescent type of pattern for social interaction. Further, the low aspiration level and realistic intellectual approach expressed in Rorschach responses is congruent with the fatalistic attitude toward the world, where achievement motives are

---

[3] In Chapter 5 there is further discussion of the native-oriented psychological structure, in comparison with that of the elite acculturated. The point is made there that the range of personality characteristics among the present native-oriented group is probably narrower and that the modal personality type is more withdrawn than for the Menomini in the prereservation period. The statements made here, however, hold good for the period for which we have direct evidence.

irrelevant and one's "success" depends solely upon the amount of power that one controls. The Rorschach, however, did not reveal other important features inferred from the analysis of ordinary behavior. For instance, autonomy, a very important feature, could not be shown directly by any of the Rorschach indicators. Materials from the Rorschach did, however, support the assumption of homogeneity existing in the native-oriented group—both cultural and psychological.

It is apparent that early explorers and missionaries and traders who were the first to contact the Menomini in the seventeenth century noticed many of the same kinds of behaviors and attitudes observed by fieldworkers from 1896 to the present. Descriptive phrases used by priests and early explorers—generous, soft-spoken, suppression of criticism in face-to-face relations, strong sense of humor, fear of sorcery—are applicable to the contemporary native-oriented Menomini. It is tempting to conclude that there has simply been a tenacious persistence of basic attitudes, values, beliefs, and psychological "set." However, this inference is subject to strong criticism by some anthropologists and ethno-historians. Some might call these apparent similarities between the Menomini of the past and the present convergences, emerging fortuitously over time. An explanation more compatible to the authors is that many of these patterned traits have continuity with the past and are kept alive because the people in the native-oriented group self-consciously choose to identify with their culture in every way possible, as a way of adapting to the impact of Western culture and the ensuing conflict and confusion. This is done by copying methods of child-rearing from grandparents, reinterpreting one's dreams to emphasize their importance in predicting the future, cautiously observing the implicit and explicit "rules" of one's grandparents for good living, and, in some cases, reviving old dances and customs such as the War Dance, which was relearned recently from the Chippewa. The psychological characteristics described do not occur in a cultural or social vacuum, or somehow magically outlast the cultural system in which they were functional. The native-oriented Menomini are as they are because an attenuated, though recognizable, native culture has been kept alive. Surely neither the culture nor the personality is an intact and complete version of the culture or personality of the past, but that there is continuity seems undeniable.

Members of the native-oriented group feel the discrepancies existing between the expectations of the more acculturated Menomini and Whites and those of their own group. The realization of these discrepancies tends to reinforce the culture patterns of the native-oriented group and gives them at times a somewhat exaggerated quality. One woman in this group, who was painfully aware of the situation, remarked:

Sometimes I think a lot about a future when I'm alone. I'm a great one to think about the future. Seems like the young children are getting worse. We was all raised different. I warn my children and try to tell them things. I gotta wait a little until they are older. I try to tell 'em things my father told me. But, they learn things from different children. I try to break them of different habits. I wonder if I'm gonna be strong enough to get 'um on my side. [L. Spindler, field notes]

The way of life of the native-oriented group can be said to represent, at least in part, a resistance or a reaffirmative movement. Its members are not, however, trying to reform the outside world, or even transform the conditions of their own existence. They are attempting to exclude certain aspects of the outside world and turn in upon what they know of their own past. Many of the members have attempted to adjust to the outside world and, upon returning, have brought strengthened commitments to the "Menomini" way. This strategy can be effective so long as there is a group of some size to maintain the cultural boundaries with sufficient man- and woman-power to fill crucial roles, such as elder, learner, transmitter, and provider, as well as specific positions in the religious organizations that are the most visible manifestations of the reaffirmation of a native-oriented way of life.

The section to follow will deal with the interplay between the behavior patterns and psychological organization of the Menomini already described and the social system in which they operate. A given kind of social system tends to select and reinforce certain kinds of psychological structures and patterns of behavior in order to make the social system work.[4] The next section of the chapter will deal with religion, subsistence activities, the structure of authority and social control, witchcraft, and ceremonial organizations that provide the framework of meanings within which the native-oriented Menomini act.

How the System Works

THE ECONOMIC BASE

Although much has changed in the environment of the Menomini during recent decades, the subsistence activities of the native-oriented group exhibit some continuity with the past. The old way of life was always one of seasonal and intermittent activity to gain a living from the forests, streams, and lakes. The Menomini had small gardens before the Whiteman came in which they grew squash, beans, and corn, but they were basically hunters and gatherers. They also made extensive use of the resources of lakes and streams, particularly of sturgeon and wild rice.

The Malhominis {are adroit} . . . in spearing the Sturgeon in their river. For this purpose they use only small Canoes, very light, in which they stand upright, and in the middle of the current spear the Sturgeon. . . . [La Potherie, 1665, in *Wisconsin Historical Collections*, Madison, Wisconsin, vol. xvi:9 cited in Keesing 1939:20]

---

[4] We are aware of the problems concerning shared motivations and the operation of social systems discussed by Anthony Wallace (1961) and others. For national systems and whole societies the problem is more significant than for this small group of native-oriented Menomini. There is variability in roles and personalities in even this group, however. In our analysis to follow we are stressing what people in this group have in common rather than the ways they are different.

Because of their horticultural and maritime habits, it was possible for them to live in villages for a part of the year, for their environment, as a rule, was quite productive during the summer months, and there was always the wild-rice harvest in the fall. During the harsh winters, however, the people probably usually resumed the nomadic hunting life that represents the basic subsistence pattern of the northern forest tribes. During this time it was not possible for large groups to live together in villages. Each extended family or small band went on its way, hunting over a territory defined by usage, and the threat of starvation was always present.

The fur trade, beginning almost immediately after the earliest contacts with the French in the latter half of the seventeenth century, caused substantial changes in the social and economic adaptation of the Menomini that will be discussed later. The small band became the basic unit, and this band was nomadic. The semisedentary seasonal village pattern declined, though the persistence of village sites into the nineteenth century suggests that the pattern was never entirely abandoned.

Today the people no longer gather in villages in the summer and fragment into nomadic bands in the winter, or roam about in fur-collecting and -trading groups, and yet their life retains a nomadic and intermittent character. Some of the men in the native-oriented group work with logging crews in the forest, but this work is dependent upon the season of the year, the depth of the snow, and the "cut" needed to keep the sawmill operating. All of the men and boys fish and hunt. Until recently most families went to pick cherries, potatoes, and strawberries, in season, for farmers and orchardists in Wisconsin and Michigan. A few baskets, paintings, bas-relief carvings, and, particularly, beadwork items are sold to tourists. Many individuals and families pick ferns and evergreen boughs. A fast worker can make $15 per day in season. A few people go to Minnesota to gather wild rice each year.

In addition to these activities, members of the group have organized themselves into a loosely defined "troupe" that performs weekly "play dances" for tourists, often traveling to various towns throughout the state.[5] In relation to the amount of time and energy expended in putting them on, they do not provide a very substantial addition to the income of this group. On three consecutive Sundays in 1958 the "take" ran between $12 and $30. This was divided so many ways that each participant received no more than $2, and usually less. This was "pay" for at least six hours of dancing in the dusty, hot arena. Obviously, the pleasure derived from the dances was more important than the money. Although a Whiteman or acculturated Menomini would have regarded the business as a failure, the members of this group seemed quite unconcerned with the amount of the gate proceeds and saw nothing foolish about going through with it week after week. One man even quit his wage job so that he could make a costume and paint some signs for the affair.

---

[5] This activity has grown in significance in recent years, and the troupe, consisting only of native-oriented individuals in 1958, now (1970) includes individuals from transitional and acculturated families.

Some members of the dance troupe from the native-oriented group in 1952. The beadwork designs, costumes, and, particularly, the roach headdress are all of the woodland type, distinctive from the Plains style, which has recently become popular.

Some of the ladies, ready for a powwow for tourists, in 1960.

Hunting is an occasional source of meat, and some men spend long hours in the woods. The dense forests of the Menomini area still shelter deer, bear, and partridge, and the many lakes float their share of ducks and occasional geese. Skill in hunting is highly valued. One man who is regarded as an excellent hunter shot thirteen bears in five years and averages about seven deer a year. The technique most used is to take position near a deer run or watering place, or sometimes by a salt lick set out to attract game. Once in position, a man may wait for his quarry for a whole day or night with hardly a movement. When food runs low, a man will go out to stay until he kills something. One man stayed out four days with only a half a loaf of bread and a pound of salt pork for provisions, but he came back with the hindquarters and hide of a bear. The man and his wife ate none of it, despite the fact that they were very hungry, and it was sold to the restaurant near Keshena, because eating bear meat would be dangerous without ritual precautions that the hunter did not have the power or knowledge to carry out. He did, however, pay his respects to the bear before he shot him. The hunter killed one bear from his platform and another appeared on the scene within a minute of the first—but the hunter did not kill this one. He coughed instead, and then shouted, "Hey, Chief, what are you doing around here?" If the bear had stayed, he would have shot him, he said, and he declared, "You know, bears aren't like deers. They are like human beings." This attitude is of long standing.

> . . . the animal or bird forms that may thus be adopted by an Indian are sometimes the same as the totem of which he is a member. Under such circumstances the animal representing the totem, and the "familiar" or ma'nido, is seldom hunted or shot; but should he be permitted to hunt such an animal the hunter will first address the animal and ask forgiveness for killing him, telling him that certain portions, which are tabu, shall be set up in the place of honor in the wikö'mik. For instance, should an Indian of the Bear totem, or one whose adopted guardian is represented by the bear, desire to go hunting and meet with that animal, due apology would be paid to it before destroying it. The carcass would then be dressed and served, but no member of the Bear totem would partake of the meat, though the members of all other totems could freely do so. The hunter could, however, eat of the paws and head, the bones of the latter being subsequently placed upon a shelf, probably over the door, or in some other conspicuous place. Due reverence is paid to such a relic of the totem, and so strictly observed is this custom that no greater insult could be offered to the host than for anyone to take down such bones and to cast them carelessly aside.
>
> Due reverence must be had by the Indian for his so-called guardian or ma'nido, neglect in this direction sometimes being considered as the direct cause of misfortune or sickness. [Hoffman 1896:64–65]

The method of hunting is in sharp contrast with that used by most White hunters, who select an area where there is good cover and a number of them "drive" the area. The frightened game moves ahead of them, to be shot by hunters posted at strategic points where they can cover a certain area. This method is foreign to the native-oriented Menomini. Each man hunts for himself. He settles down and waits for the game to appear rather than forcing it out. When he kills, the meat is not distributed piecemeal to all the members of the group, or even to his relatives. His in-laws, if nearby, will receive a sizeable chunk. If there is a seasonal rite for the Dream Dance or a meeting of the Medicine Lodge, he will contribute his meat to feed the participants, but otherwise, he and his immediate family consume it as rapidly as possible.

Life in this mode has its ups and downs. People still go hungry, though almost no one starves today.[6] From the Whiteman's point of view, however, there is little security. There is rarely food in the house for more than a very few days ahead. No one has freezers or food storage lockers, and work is intermittent. The typical pattern is to work hard at cherry picking or greens gathering for a few weeks. When that is finished, there is money for food and a few bottles of beer for awhile. Then there is no point in working. Work in itself has no value. There is nothing to "get ahead" toward, from their point of view. As long as there is enough to eat, things are fine, and when the food runs out, something "always comes along," if one can wait long enough to see what it will be.

The values and attitudes and psychological organization described here are functional in this setting. Equanimity under duress is a good quality to possess in an intermittent and seminomadic subsistence economy. Autonomy is apparent in the lack of organized cooperation in economic endeavor. Latescence makes it possible for one to wait for the game to come rather than drive it out, or to wait expectantly, rarely hopelessly, for the next thing to turn up that will put food in the pot. It is not necessary to live this way in present-day Wisconsin, but if they did not live this way, the native-oriented Menomini would cease being native oriented. It is their way of life and has continuity with the past.

SOCIAL ORGANIZATION AS RELATED TO THE ECONOMIC BASE

The social organization of the Menomini has undergone some rather drastic shifts over the centuries as shifts in the economic base have occurred. The transitions have been from a more sedentary village-type existence to a large-scale hunting (for furs) economy to the reservation-type economic patterns. And now (1970) the terminal phases of adaptation to non-ward status and to the problems of survival in a competitive economy are in process. (This is dealt with briefly in Chapter 6.)

Early records refer to the tribe, or a portion of it, as living in a "village" at Menominee River (Keesing 1939:34). This village type of life was based on a fishing and wild-rice economy. Early documents and origin myths of the Menomini point to the existence of a dual organization or moiety system defined

---

[6] "Almost" is correct, for in 1965 one man, living in an isolated cabin and ill, died of a combination of his ills and malnutrition.

as the Thunderers and Bears, with subdivisions into patrilineal totemic[7] descent groups[8] and some larger groupings in phratries[9] (Keesing 1939:38).

> *The Bear {came out of the ground and} . . . was made an Indian. . . . He found himself alone, and decided to call to himself Kineʼu, the Eagle, and said, "Eagle, come to me and be my brother." Thereupon the eagle descended, and also took the form of a human being. While they were considering whom to call upon to join them, they perceived a beaver approaching. The Beaver . . . was adopted as a younger brother of the Thunderer. . . . {Then} the Sturgeon . . . was adopted by the Bear as a younger brother and servant. . . . The Elk was accepted by the Thunderer as a younger brother and watercarrier . . . {and} the Crane and the Wolf became younger brothers of the Bear {also the Dog and Deer which were associated with the Wolf in a sub-group}. . . . The Good Mystery made the Thunderers the laborers . . . {and} also gave {them} corn . . . {They} were also makers of fire. . . .*
>
> *The Thunderers decided to visit the Bear village {at the Menominee river} . . . and when they arrived at that place they asked the Bear to join them, promising to give corn and fire in return for {wild} rice, which was the property of the Bear and Sturgeon. . . . The Bear family agreed to this, and since that time the two families have therefore lived together.* [From the sacred origin myth in Hoffman 1896:39–41]

Exogamy [marriage outside the clan (or the older term "gens")] was required and polygyny (one man married to two or more women) was accepted.

> *Marriage outside of the gens was imperative, and disregard of this rule would have been incest, because of the putative relationship of all those claiming descent from the same totem. Violations of the rule are said to have been unknown in old days.* [From a reconstruction by Skinner 1913:19]

Kinship terminology, and the behaviors associated with it, are apparently of long standing. The system of terminology is largely classificatory (lumping specified sets of relatives together under one term); in this case, for example, father and father's brother are given one term. Father's brother's children or mother's sister's children (parallel cousins)[10] are given the same terms as brothers and sisters. Some of the other outstanding features of the system are as follows: (1) Distinctions are made between parallel and cross-cousins (mother's brother's children or father's sister's children). (2) Nephews and nieces are important on either side.

---

[7] A descent relationship, in this case through the male line, to a presumed animal ancestor.

[8] These may be regarded as clans since descent from a remote and fictive ancestor is the basis for relationship.

[9] A union of two or more clans for social or ceremonial purposes.

[10] See E. Schusky, *Manual for Kinship Analysis* (revised edition, 1971) for a glossary of kinship terms and an explanation of the principles of kinship systems.

A person's nephews, nieces, and brothers- and sisters-in-law are his closest relations next to the parents, nearer even than an actual blood brother or sister. If a man goes to war his nephew, on either side, or his brother-in-law, must follow him regardless of any hindrance. This is a great point of honor, and most strictly observed. The nephew must act as a servant to him and protect him from danger at the risk of his own life. If the uncle is killed his nephew must get a scalp from the enemy in revenge, or never come home alive. In a like manner the nephew is his uncle's blood avenger, should the uncle be slain in an intertribal quarrel. Nephews and nieces are greatly indulged by their uncles and aunts, who refuse them nothing for which they ask, no matter how costly it may be, or how inconvenient. It would be a great disgrace to do so. [From Skinner's reconstructions from elderly informants, 1913:20]

(3) Restraints are observed in the parents-in-law relationships.

A man may never speak to his mother-in-law, and must be respectfully silent in her presence. Though there is no fixed rule to this effect, the same thing is usually observed in the case of his father-in-law. To the father-in-law belong certain privileges in dividing his son-in-law's game. In the case of a bear, he skins the animal and keeps the skin, one side, the head and neck, while his son-in-law gets the other side and all four quarters. This rule is not followed in regard to any other game. [From Skinner's reconstructions of the old culture, 1913:20]

(4) Prescribed joking relationships exist between certain classes of relatives.

The joking-relationship exists between a person and his uncles and aunts, nephews and nieces, sisters-in-law and brothers-in-law, on either side, but is strictly tabooed between cousins. Any joke, no matter how rough, is permissible, and so is sexual intercourse. [Skinner 1913:20]

Hereditary chiefs—heads of descent groups—with the chief of the Bear group as tribal chief, were included in the formal social structure of the pre-contact Menomini. The lineage chiefs probably constituted a village council and regulated civil affairs to a limited extent. Aside from this civil leadership there were said to be chiefs who won prestige through individual dreams or due to their special prowess. Those persons acted as keepers of the war medicines and as public spokesmen for hereditary leaders, and as masters of ceremonies during public celebrations (Keesing 1939:40). In spite of certain formal structures of control, it is probable that the Menomini and other tribes in the area had little secular authority exercised by any leader. The Menomini were described by the Jesuit Father Allouez as a people who "have neither laws, nor police, nor magistrates to check disorder" (quoted from Keesing 1939:40). The problem of social control will be dealt with later in the chapter.

Materials given here regarding the groupings and their organization and functions is inferential to a large degree. The system began to disintegrate in the seventeenth century, and there are contradictions in the materials of early students such as Hoffman and Skinner. There is agreement, however, as to the general outline of the totemic descent groups but disagreement as to the specific names and number of groupings.

After the French fur traders arrived (1667), readjustments in the social system were necessary. The Menomini became primarily hunters and trappers. The older village and clan system broke down and the "band" system emerged to meet the demands of the new fur-trading economy. By 1830 there were nine bands. All of the able-bodied Menomini set out by canoe along the inland rivers for the fall and winter hunt. Since large groupings would not be feasible under these conditions, families ranged in congenial groups. As the forest areas nearby became denuded of game, the groups had to go farther, and each then tended to claim customary rights over a given river path and hunting territory; because of the credit system, the fur traders sent agents along with the band. During the summer months the Menomini camped at places convenient for fishing and making gardens, and gathering maple syrup, berries, and wild rice. These groups tended to remain stable, with the summer sites located near the fall canoes routes. Bands were primarily friendship groups, but tended to follow clan lines. Later the distinctiveness broke down, but some of the bands retained strong clan marks up to the reservation period. The small family or household group fit into the band organization as well as it had the village type. Monogamy became more prevalent. There were more men, as there was less warrior mortality, and the monogamous family was a less unwieldy canoe-and-hunting-trip group. The individual family grew in importance in the loosely knit band system, and this trend toward individualism has continued to the present among the native oriented. Kinship behaviors and terms of address were little changed by this shift to band organization.

Modifications occurred, however, in the tribal leadership. Certain new standards for leaders included success in obtaining furs, directing hunting and trading operations, and obtaining credit, in ability to orate, and in getting along well with Whites and other Indian tribes. A new institution in the form of a tribal council came into being which was to grow in importance. Frequent tribal council and inter tribal councils were held. Ability to excel in formal oratory was a great asset for a leader at the council meetings, and continued to be so until contemporary times.

When the Menomini reservation was formed in 1852, a sedentary-type subsistence was required, and the band system of the fur-trading era began to distintegrate. The various band leaders, it is said, chose locations that appealed to them on the reserve, and the members of their bands either grouped themselves nearby or selected other areas where they and their families might live. However, the band type of organization did not entirely disappear. Peoples regrouped in congenial cooperative groups under different leaders and were still called bands. When these new bands became settled and less isolated from other groups, they in turn tended to lose their unity (Keesing 1939:150). The old totemic dualism seemed to persist in the division of the tribe into "Christians" and "pagans." Those following the traditional religion also divided into two groups more or less based on the old division of Bear and Thunderer. When some families started to farm and others began to log, a variety of regroupings occurred to fit the environmental demands of the particular subsistence technique. Members of the contemporary native-oriented group live in and around Zoar, where they have resided since the early reservation period. They are often referred to as the pagan group by others. The area is surrounded by dense woods and streams, which make it possible for some members of the group to continue to hunt and fish in Menomini fashion. The social organization remains similar today to that found in the early reservation period.

Many of the older members of the native-oriented group have a totem or clan affiliation. It was common practice until very recently for each individual to have his totem painted, usually upside down, on a grave stick at his place of burial. Some marriages are still arranged by elders. The kinship terminology described by Skinner in 1913 is still in use in the Menomini tongue (mixed with Potawatomi and Chippewa terms) and is frequently projected indirectly into the English kinship usage, as, for instance, when referring to a parallel cousin, in such phrases as "He is like a brother to me." The same term is used for father and father's brother, for mother's father and father's father, and distinctions are still made between cross-cousins and parallel cousins. All of the people around Zoar are conscious of kin relationships to each other, and this has created a powerful force pulling them together into a cohesive group. The exact relationships are not always clear in the minds of some of the younger people. They will often declare that they know they are "close" to so-and-so but are not able to explain just in what way. One man remarked, "We're all related here at Zoar but we don't always know just how. Only the old people know."

Some of the old obligations and prerogatives between relatives have been retained. The old joking relationships, particularly between a man and his brother-in-law, are very much alive, as shown in the behavior examples given previously. The outsider coming into the situation is shocked, at first, by the ribald attacks on another man's character, origins, house, and family, committed under the sanctions of this system, that seem so out of place among an otherwise restrained people. Other kinship obligations survive in the distribution of meat killed in hunting and the understanding that certain relatives, when called upon, must provide economic help in time of distress, or when a candidate is being "put up" for the Medicine Lodge.

Elders are still the most respected persons in the group. Great powers are attributed to elders, and all are potential witches. This is the group from which the leadership is drawn. The elders know the ritual of the Medicine Lodge and Dream Dance, are in direct contact with the supernatural powers, can prophesy with their dreams, can name a child appropriately, and are the authorities for questions on kin relationships. No man under sixty could pretend to much knowledge or experience in these matters, but not all men over sixty are leaders. Positions of prestige and leadership are a function of age, inheritance, and amount of sacred power controlled by the person. During the decade under consideration, the elder with greatest authority was in his seventies, but he was also the son of one of the last of the true shamans, did curing with both charms and herbs, and was known as the only man resident in the native-oriented community who could honestly claim to have gone successfully through the major puberty fast and achieved his power through a vision. His leadership was threatened only by an elderly woman, who is a lineal descendant of chiefs and is regarded as a powerful witch. This system of symbols and sanctions represents little fundamental change from that of the old culture but is in sharp contrast to that operating for the rest of the Menomini community.

The exercise of authority is much like that described by the Jesuits and fur traders two centuries ago. As mentioned earlier, Nicholas Perrote, the fur trader, wrote: "The father does not venture to exercise authority over his son, nor does the chief dare to give commands to his soldier. . . ." Social control for this group will be discussed in a later section in connection with witchcraft.

THE WORLD AROUND THEM: MENOMINI COSMOLOGY

All them [spirits above] what God created is good. And there is some awe·toks [spirits] that isn't good; belong someplace else . . . under the ground. [Menomini informant, in Slotkin 1957:26]

The earth is believed to be an island, floating in an illimitable ocean, separating the two halves of the universe into an upper and a lower portion, regarded as the above of the benevolent and the malevolent powers, respectively. Each portion is divided into four superimposed tiers, inhabited by supernatural beings, the power of whom increases in ratio to their remoteness from the earth. [Skinner 1921:29]

And this we call awe·tok, this sun, that brings the light every day. . . . They even put up tobacco [for the sun]; . . . This sun here, he's got lots of power. He watches over the Indians, too. Sometimes he gives them power [as a guardian spirit]. . . . Sometimes that ke·soʔ [sun] would give them power so they could see at night. [Menomini informant, in Slotkin 1957:28]

In the highest tier above the earth resides the deity to whom all others are subordinate. The testimony of the early writers is unanimous that this being was the sun. . . . [Skinner 1921:29]

. . . the Great Spirit saw the Indians, his people; he did not like what was happening; the Indian being killed; those spirits killing him; all kinds of animals killing him. That great spirit, the Great Spirit, thought it over. This is what he thought, one time: "Well, instead I will make some ones to watch over these, my children the Indians. I will make them." . . . Then he probably made the Thunderbirds. He put them over here; he put them everywhere. He put the Thunderbirds, large birds, to watch over these Indians; . . . They would speak to them, and feed them, in order that the Thunderbirds should look after them carefully, so that they might be allowed to live well. That everything would grow abundantly here, for them to eat; that the Thunderbirds would water [everything] with the water they carry—that it would rain properly so that everything would be wet—that is what the old people probably would pray for. [Menomini informant, in Slotkin 1957:27]

Beneath the supreme being, in descending order, . . . are three tiers of bird-like deities. First . . . come the Thunderbirds, gods of war. [Skinner 1921:30]

They [the stars] just watch over everything in the night. Just like that [Indian] policeman; maybe that's why he got that star [shaped badge]. He's taking care of people. If they do something wrong, well, he can go and put them someplace [i.e., in jail] . . . wa·pananah [morning star] is some kind of a chief of all stars, head one. When he comes out, it's getting daylight. [Menomini informant, in Slotkin 1957:30]

In the eastern sky dwells morning star, often personified as a man of large stature, with an enormous mouth. Morningstar frequently appears to young men in their dreams with promises of strength and success. He, too, has influence in martial affairs, and with the sun, was one of the joint donors of the war bundle through the thunderbirds. [Skinner 1913:81]

1st informant: The Bear is one who lived over here in the Underground Place; that is the White Bear. White Bear is the one underground who holds up the earth. He is also one whom the Great Spirit thought about, who himself holds up the [sky] above, over here. They speak to each other back and forth, the Great Spirit and White Bear; they tell each other something. That is the way those two work; they are alike.

2nd informant: . . . they say that he has got as much power as Great Spirit got; he's got lots of power, too. And he's taking charge of everything here. Them berries what's growing in the woods, all the berries, he owns that; he's taking charge of that so they come up good. [Slotkin 1957:32–33]

Beneath the earth, there is, in the lowest tier, the Great White Bear with a long copper tail, who, in addition to being the chief and patron of all earthly bears and the traditional ancestor of the Menomini tribe, is the principal power for evil. [Skinner 1921:30–31]

1st informant: That Hairy Serpent is one who is not good. . . . That is the one that sometimes swims by [like a water snake], too. . . . He would swing his tail at him [i.e., an Indian in a boat] on the top of the water, so that he would capsize; then he would capture him. Therefore he is not good, that Hairy Serpent. [translation]

2nd informant: Mi·?s-kenu·pik is in every lake. It must be one [in the lake] over here, down the hill there; there's a lake there. And [in] every lake there's a mi·?s-kenu·pik; that's where he is. Even in the rivers; we see them [in a] spring, little creeks, towards that river. He comes out that way. [Slotkin 1957:32]

During the Spindlers' period of fieldwork Horned Hairy Serpent was reported seen in a lake near Keshena. Four men, returning from fishing, said they saw something big in the water and rowed near until they saw that it was a tremendous serpent. They shot at it, with no effect. They were so frightened that they jumped out of the boat and ran as soon as they came to shallow water. After a day or two a party of men went back to investigate. They saw nothing but found a track on the road where the huge serpent had apparently dragged himself across the dirt. Some nonbelievers said that the "only serpent those guys saw was in a bottle," and that "some jokers must have dragged a sack of sand around to make tracks." Rumors of *mi·ʔs-kenu·pik* still persist today (1970).

The horned snake is the best known of these evil animals because he is nearest to, and consequently most frequently seen on, the earth. The great horned serpents, or as they are more often called, Mīsikinūbikuk, "hairy snakes," are gigantic reptiles with bodies of the usual form, but covered with black or golden scales, while on their hairy heads grow stag-like horns. They seek to destroy man, and come above the ground to search for him whenever they dare, but in this effort they are rarely successful, owing to their relentless enemies, the thunderbirds. For a Menomini to see one of these snakes in his waking hours is a bad sign, perhaps foretelling death in his family; to see one in a dream is an evil omen and the dreamer, if he has been fasting for a vision, should at once break his fast and start it a second time. Should he accept the vision, he becomes possessed of the malign powers of sorcery and witchcraft.

A sorcerer often claims to possess a scale or a portion of the flesh of one of these serpents which he keeps carefully hidden in one of his medicine bags to use in practising witchcraft. It is well known to the Menomini that isolated and lonely hills, ponds, swamps, or sloughs are apt to be the homes of these monsters. [Skinner 1913:81–82]

The Giant is one who is not good; he is not good. That Giant wants the Indian; he kills him in order to eat him. He eats them, that Giant. [Menomini informant, in Slotkin 1957:34]

In the north, whence the cold winds blow, there dwells at the end of the earth a race of malevolent giants {mänupäwuk . . .} driven there by Mä'näbus {Menomini culture here} because of their desire to destroy mankind. That they may not return during his absence Mä'näbus has made an ocean separating their country from the rest of the earth and mankind. When the south winds blow, the odor of human flesh is borne to their nostrils and they attempt to wade the watery barrier. But it is too deep even for their magnificent size, and they soon give it up. That they may never swim to the other shore, Mä'näbus has thoughtfully created gigantic bloodsuckers or leeches which attack the giants and drive them back. [Skinner 1913:83]

. . . *pe·hcekona·h* [sacred bundle] is the same one as *pe·hcekona·h nɛ·yo·htah* [the one who carries a sacred bundle on his back] . . . he is a spirit. That is why I say that I myself am afraid of everything. Well, this *pe·hcekona·h*, as he is called, is a great spirit; some time ago he was a person; that is what he was in the past. . . . When he tells someone that something is going to happen —he warns them . . . they feel his very presence. That is how much of a spirit he is, that *pe·hcekona·h*. That is why it is really hard to talk about him. Wait until tonight; I myself will offer tobacco to that *pe·hcekona·h*. [The informant is a sorcerer. Translation, in Slotkin 1957:34.]

The "wandering man" {Petcikunau naiota, "Bundle Carrier,"} is an individual bearing a burden ceaselessly over the face of the earth. He sometimes lingers in one locality for a long time, and then he may not be heard of again for years. He rarely appears to anyone save to foretell misfortune; but he is not infrequently heard by travelers as he rustles along through the leaves or bushes at night. A gift of tobacco or liquor will cause him to go way. If he is angered, he will pursue the person who has offended him, and even throw sticks at the fugitive. To be hit with a stick thrown by the "wandering man" means death. To defeat him in a wrestling match is most propitious and means long life and happiness. [Skinner 1913:83]

George Spindler reported to a group of Menomini a dream about some tiny Indians sitting on the crosspieces of the inner supports of the Spindlers' tent and poking holes in the roof with their spears. He shouted at them in his dream, but they kept right on poking holes. This was serious, because it was raining hard! As the episode was told, everyone nearby listening became silent and stayed so for a few minutes. After a while one of the men said, "George, you know who them little guys was?" "No, do you?" "Well, them's the Little God Boys. They stick around, pester you like that. But don't do nothin' to scare them off. They're good to have around. They look after you. Just cause you trouble in little ways."

The "little god boys" are pygmies who dwell particularly at "death's Door" on Lake Michigan. They are friendly to men. One of their most remarkable qualities is the power to pass through stone as though it did not exist. [Skinner 1913:83–84]

Well, that is why I exist. . . . It is because of my soul [*nete·ʔcyak*] that I live. If something should happen to me, then it leaves, and I die.
My soul is that which travels all night; that soul of mine walks [then]. Well, this one is always right here; it stay here in my body, that one, my soul. There are two souls of mine. One travels at night. This one right here maintains me; it is right here. That soul of mine is the one that is like a shadow [*kawe·hseh*]. [Translation, in Slotkin 1957:44–45]

While we were interviewing two ladies near their homes, some distance back in the woods, one old man, known to be irascible, approached George Spindler. "You smart Whiteman. How many souls does a man have?" George Spindler replied "Only one," thinking that the old man, quite drunk, would be only angered by an "Indian" reply from a Whiteman. But the old man shouted, "You God damned Whiteman! You think this Indian is dumb! He is smarter than you damn Whitemen. A man has two souls, one here [he struck his forehead], and one here [he struck his chest]." With that he stomped off to his house, shouting over his shoulder. George Spindler asked one of his sons, standing nearby, "What did he say?" "He says he is going to kill you!" George Spindler circled the house and looked in the window. There on the floor lay old Peˑsek, passed out. Under him lay his shotgun. The fieldworkers left shortly, taking the ladies with them to finish interviewing elsewhere.

> ... *every human being is possessed of two souls. One, called usually agawétätciuk {"a shade across"} resides in the head. This is the intellect, and after death it wanders about aimlessly, lingering about the graveyard. It is for these spirits that sacrifices of food are offered. They are ghosts as differentiated from souls....*
>
> *The soul, or tcebai, dwells in the heart and is the one which travels to the hereafter. It is the tcebai for which all funeral services are held.* [Skinner 1913:85]

First they go down this way [pointing west]. And that fellow over there [Naˑhpaʔtɛh], he knows what kind of a person this is. Maybe he [had] been killing people by witchbag and stuff like that, suffered people [i.e., made people suffer], he [Naˑhpaʔtɛh] tells him what road to follow. And he comes to kind of a swamp, like, you know, water and lots of mud. That's where he drives them kind of people, and they're going to suffer there a long time. And the good people, that fellow takes them there [to the Abode of the Dead], and fix them up good. But bad people, he don't take them [there]. [Slotkin 1957:46]

It appears that the cognitive world of the contemporary native-oriented Menomini remains similar to that of the Menomini when the traditional culture was yet intact during the time of Skinner's early work and even to early contact times. The beliefs concerning the ordering of the sky beings, those of the earth, and those of the underworld remain similar even in detail, and the fear of the evil spirits on all sides is still pervasive today. As a most-powerful shaman said of one of the spirits (peˑhcekonaˑh," the bundle carrier"), "That is why I say that I myself am afraid of everything. . . . Wait until tonight; I myself will offer tobacco to that peˑhcekonaˑh." Another inference that can be drawn is that the Menomini belief system is dualistic, with continuous cosmic conflict between the good spirits above the earth and the evil spirits below.[11] With the world and the heavens and the underworld peopled with such spectacular, often dangerous, beings, it is not surprising that most of the religious observances of the contemporary group and those reported by the early explorers and missionaries are

---

[11] The extent to which this dualism is a result of Christian influence remains a puzzle. Probably, the concept was reinforced by the Christian cosmology, but the dualism in Menomini thinking is different. Good and evil are not absolutes, and any one spiritual entity, person, or thing may have attributes of both.

those concerned with securing and maintaining supernatural power, partly as protection against evil forces. Another inference to be drawn is that there is no real separation between man and animal in the Menomini belief system. Figures in the puberty dream appear in either animal or human form. Witches can take the form of an animal. As the Rorschachs also showed, the concept of the peopled universe for the Menomini is zoomorphic rather than anthropomorphic.

Powerful men and women who control both good and evil powers have always been held in awe by the Menomini. In earlier times people were identified who were primarily "witches" performing evil acts and who had received one of the underworld spirits as a tutelary in a vision, but these were very few in number. Usually, a shaman was and is able to control both good and evil forces. Until rather recent times, shamans in special groups spent a large portion of their time combating evil powers exercised by witches or those possessing an "evil bag" made up of parts of animals representing underworld spirits (owl skins, bear claws, and so forth). The earlier religious groupings included the Wa·beno and the Cese·ko or Jugglers. These shamans worked more or less entirely as individuals (Keesing 1939:50). None of the authors' informants had direct knowledge of the Wa·beno cult, whose members claimed the Morning Star or the Sun as their tutelary spirit. They were said to be able to furnish hunting medicine, prescribe herbal remedies, and sell love powders and charms which would cause an indifferent person to fall in love with the owner. They claimed a special immunity to fire and boiling water.

The Cese·ko, or Jugglers as they were called by the early writers, persisted until the first quarter of the twentieth century. They were diviners and doctors of great powers who worked in a special lodge when they consulted the spirits to cure the sick. The small birch bark lodge swayed from side to side (thus the term "shaking-tent rite" is often applied); wind was heard, and voices spoke to the seer. The Cese·ko supposedly replied through the medium of the turtle, who acted as an interviewer. It was the role of the Cese·ko to find out the cause of the patient's illness, which was usually witchcraft since disease was unnatural. The Cese·ko would then attempt to coax the soul of the patient to return and enter a small wooden cylinder, where it was imprisoned and delivered to its relatives. The cylinder was then attached to the patient's breast for four days so that the soul could return to his body. If the patient had been wounded by a witch's arrow, the Cese·ko proceeded to extract the arrow by sucking through a bone tube. He then vomited forth the arrow, displayed it to the onlookers, and announced that the patient was cured. The witch's arrow was usually found to be a maggot, a fly, a quill, or some other small object. (See Skinner 1921:72.)

Several living Menomini in the native-oriented group have witnessed a shaking-tent rite:

I seen him, J., shake a tepee by Dutchman's tower. It was just three poles stuck around and canvas around it. He was supposed to doctor someone. He had three tepees and got in one and called his spirits and wanted them to get this person who was witchin' this woman. They hears his voice—the witch—and he started shakin' each tepee as fast as he could. He went in one at a time; you couldn't see him—and shook them as fast as he could. He asked the man if he was gonna quit hurtin' the woman and the man said if they left him alone, he would. I wasn't supposed to see it; I was too little about twenty-five years ago. They had one in Flambeau and Moe Lake lately. That woman was real sick. They brought her in on a stretcher. It was a scary outfit; you could hear that man's voice way up in the air—the one who was doin' the witchin'. [Menomini woman, in L. Spindler, field notes]

The values, attitudes, and psychological organization described earlier for the native-oriented Menomini are congruent with this belief system. Keeping in touch with the deities by gaining special powers is crucial in order to survive in this world peopled with spirits and monsters. The latescent, expectant attitude is appropriate for a person waiting for power to be bestowed. And each person must keep himself under control at all times lest he anger a malevolent spirit or an elder with special powers. In securing power or in using one's special powers, each person behaves autonomously. He or she has a special kind of power unique to him or her and gained in a unique fashion. As mentioned earlier, even the shamans in special cults such as the *Ceseꞏko* worked as individuals, with their own interpretations of the phenomena at hand and their own manner of performance in dealing with it.

POWER: GETTING AND MAINTAINING IT

What Is Power—What Does It Look Like?

Power is white, like when the sun is shining. Like that [pointing to a sunbeam], see; that's a power, see? . . . When God [translation of *Keseꞏmaneto′w*] wants to do anything, it goes; he's got power in him. He's the only one that got power. And *tataꞏhkesewen*, that means power [too]. [Male informant, in Slotkin 1957:25]

According to Menomini elders, power is an immaterial and invisible force that gives off a bright light. "It produces characteristic effects in things which are subjected to it, and can be transformed from one thing to another. People who do not have power are ineffective and weak; once they obtain such power, they become effective and strong." The Menomini used three terms interchangeably for power: *tataꞏhkesewen* (that which has energy), *meꞏskowesan* (that which has strength), and *ahpeꞏhtesewen* (that which is valuable) (Slotkin 1957:25).

How Does a Person Gain Power?

Until recently, every normally socialized Menomini went through the *mesaꞏhkateweꞏw* (Great Fast) at puberty. Preparation for the Great Fast began during early childhood with short fasts of a day or two and instruction in the properly humble state of mind. When the individual felt ready for the ordeal and had received proper instructions from an elder, he or she went off, with a charcoal-blackened face, into the woods, to a tiny bark wigwam already constructed for this purpose.

They are taught from the age of four or five years to blacken their faces, to fast, and to dream . . . being led to believe that thus they will be successful in fishing, hunting, and war. [A seventeenth century Jesuit missionary in *Jesuit Relations* 1896–1901, vol. lvii:265–287]

One stayed alone, quite cut off from all human contact, and with no food for periods ranging up to ten days or even two weeks or longer. During this time the initiate was supposed to banish all thoughts from the mind except those concerned with the purpose of the fast—to receive a vision and through this experience find the source of the power, in the form of a guardian spirit, that would guide and keep him through his whole lifetime. His attitude must be humble, supplicatory, so that the powers will take pity on him and notify him of their interest. If he is successful, the Golden Eagle, the White Bear, the Buffalo, or one of the many other spirit powers that reside in one of the layers above the earth, usually but not always in animal form, would appear before him. The Golden Eagle would take the supplicant on his back and fly over the forests and lakes, pointing out natural features that are significant in Menomini mythology. The Buffalo might chase him over rough terrain to the point of exhaustion, and he would fall face down into a sacred pool from which he might drink the source of life. If he was unsuccessful, he might either receive no notification from the spirits or be visited by one of the creatures inhabiting the strata below the earth, such as the Horned Hairy Serpent. If unsuccessful, he tried again after a lapse of some time. If he was visited by one of the underworld creatures for the fourth time, he was doomed to live a tragic life as a witch that used bad medicines to harm others, or as one who some day would murder a loved one.

After I had fasted eight days a tall man with a big red mouth appeared from the east. The solid earth bent under his steps as though it was a marsh. He said, "I have pity on you. You shall live to see your own gray hairs, and those of your children. You shall never be in danger if you make yourself a war club, such as I have and always carry it with you wherever you go. When you are in trouble, pray to me and offer me tobacco. Tobacco is what pleases me." When he had said this he vanished. [This was Morning Star. Menomini informant, in Skinner 1913:44.]

Visions often came to a girl in the form of the sun or the wind and insured qualities such as long life and happiness, unless an evil spirit came as a visitation, imbuing the girl with special evil power (L. Spindler 1970).

What happened during the Great Fast determined to a considerable degree what the initiate would be in his or her present lifetime. Whether a man would be a good hunter, a ceremonial leader, whether a woman would be a good mother and wife, or a witch, was decided by the events at that time. The person's access to the power pool through a guardian spirit—the all-permeating, universal sacred power in living things and inanimate objects alike—was defined at this time.

Today there is only one person in the group who had the Great Fast and received its benefits, though until very recently there were a number of old people still living who had. One elderly medicine man remarked during an interview:

> Hardly nobody ever has that now [the Great Fast]. K., who is older than I, had the big fast. I went to school when I was about five years old. If anyone else says they had that, they are not speaking true. K. is all there is who had it, now living. That is all. *Naha·w*! [Translation, in G. Spindler, field notes]

A woman informant in her late thirties remarked:

> Both me and my brother were supposed to fast when punished. We couldn't fast the four days. We couldn't do it. [L. Spindler, field notes]

Sister M. Inez Hilger, Benedictine sister, who worked with the Menomini in 1936, had several informants who had fasted. One relates:

> My great-grandmother fasted for forty days to receive her power. She used to tell me how she had made a hammock of tanned deerhide and had fastened it between trees on a hill, deep in the woods. She lay in this hammock fasting from all food. Whatever physical strength she received, she imbibed from the sun. Whenever she would tell me of her fast, she would say that after the forty days there was nothing left to her body but her bones and the skin over them. It was at this time that the humming bird became her medicine [*equated with tutelary spirit*]. Whenever I saw her use her medicine bag, I looked for the stuffed humming bird in it. I fasted only ten days. [Italics mine] [Hilger 1960:55]

In spite of the present situation, the pattern of securing a guardian spirit remains an integral part of the culture both in spirit and in specific form. All adults in the group had fasted for short periods as children. Some received notifications from the spirits in these preparatory fasts and ritually observe the relationship thus formed. Others have inherited both the powers and obligations of ritual observance from departed relatives.

> Like the buffalo, not so many here have been given power by them. Or like longhorn steers. You fast, and sleep, and come to in the dream. You see a longhorn coming. This longhorn chases you all over. All over the country. Like one story, a fellow told me. This fellow he run all over the country trying to elude it. Finally he see a pool, he's thirsty, played out. So he think, "If I let him get me, he can get me right here." Well then the longhorn steer come right up to him when he's laying there drinking water. He sees his image, his hair is all white. The steer, instead of hurting him, tells him, "That's what I'm trying to tell you! You drink that."
> It tastes like whiskey. Then the pool turned into a wooden bowl. That fellow, he thinks about that. Now he has to use whiskey in the future. He takes a half-pint, pours it in the wooden bowl. Then he drinks it like cattle would, and offers tobacco. After he drinks it, he turns it over with his head

like a cattle would. Whoever succeeds, gets the tobacco. I got to do that too, from my father, it comes down. [He inherited the long-horned steer as a tutelary spirit] [G. Spindler, field notes]

For the Menomini dreaming is and was a very significant activity. No dream is casually dismissed. Aside from the dreaming done during the fast periods, night dreams quite frequently carry great import.

Among . . . Menomini . . . , regular "night-dreams" have much importance. For instance, a man may dream of drowning, or of being saved from drowning, in which case he makes and always carries about with him a small canoe as a talisman. [Skinner 1913:47]

The individual usually tries to find the meaning in the dream, but if he is unsuccessful, he talks about it with an elder, who has great powers and who, by virtue of his nearness to the end of life, is close to what we would call the "supernatural." The interpretations placed on the dream experience can foretell a significant event, provide revelation concerning life, death, and sacred powers, or dictate a specific course of action ranging from how to make a special drum-stick or beadwork design to how to prevent one's husband from running off with another woman. The following is a dream from a young woman whose close relatives possessed great power and who wished to keep the Dream Dance intact, observing their prescribed code of ethics which taboos excessive drinking. This prophetic dream tells of the recent deaths of men who had drunk too much:

You know, I had a funny dream that told all about them people who died here. The children and I was looking for W. [husband] and we came to a place where we heard a lot of noise and looked in. There was a bunch of men playin' some kind of a game. They was all sittin' around a big table. In the middle was three jugs; one was marked "whiskey," one "wine," and one "beer." And each time someone would win, they would pour him a drink from one of the jugs. I saw W. sittin' there and I got scared and got him away from that table. At that table was all those people who died—W., S., N., and X., the only one who didn't die. He was drinkin' a lot at that time. All of them later died of drinkin' and I began to wonder. I wonder about X. now. [Menomini woman, in L. Spindler, field notes]

Even songs are acquired in dreams. In fact, most significant innovative behavior or important individual decision making among native-oriented Menomini is based on a dream experience and its interpretation.

They look upon their dreams as ordinances and irrevocable decrees, the execution of which it is not permitted without crime to delay. . . . A dream will take away from them sometimes their whole year's provisions. It pre-scribes their feasts, their dances, their songs, their games,—in a word, the dream does everything. [A seventeenth century report, in *Jesuit Relations* 1896–1901, vol. x:169–171]

The dream experience is a dramatic example of the difference between the cognitive world of the native-oriented Menomini and that of the Whiteman, with his rationalistic-objective view of the universe. For the Menomini the separation between mind and body, man and animal, spiritual forces and material forces, natural and supernatural is absent in their framework of belief and rationality. If the fieldworker uses the term "vision" to describe what the Menomini sees and experiences when talking to a spirit, he is gently corrected. The Menomini would say, "A Whiteman might say that, but this was no 'vision,' this happened." The term "dream" is more acceptable, for they have had many dreams and know that one is directly involved with the events in a dream—that they seem real, so real that even Whites listening to the accounts wonder if they really happened.

To be a part of the native-oriented group one must literally be a "dreamer" (passive, receptive, quiescent), and the autonomous character of the relationship between individuals and "power" is apparent. Each has his or her own experiences and carries out his or her own rituals. It is also apparent that the ability to retain one's equanimity under duress is functional in the requirement to fast in isolation. While the Great Fast is no longer possible, the short fasts required of young children reinforce this ability.

How Does a Menomini Maintain and Protect His Power?

One must observe the power rituals connected with one's tutelary spirit or special powers. Drinking whiskey in a wooden bowl while crouched on one's knees on the floor is a good example, quoted earlier, of observing ritual for a long-horned steer or buffalo tutelary spirit.

After having fasted for an indefinite period, not longer than ten days, the supplicant is approached by a being who addresses him and promises its aid and patronage for life, exacting a pledge that the dreamer will remember to make certain sacrifices from time to time in its honor and keep about his person some token of the meeting. [Skinner 1913:44]

Women have special taboos to observe during menstruation and following childbirth, when they are considered a threat to the power of the male or small child. A woman is isolated during these periods, using her own utensils, refraining from touching herself or looking up, which might offend the gods above. If a man eats food prepared by her at these times, he is in danger of losing his guardian spirit, which lives inside him, in the form of a tiny turtle or fish. If he finds out about the woman's condition in time, he can take an emetic and vomit the food before it kills the little animal. Menstruating women are careful not to feed, touch, or even breathe upon a small child for fear of causing its death. A small child may be a powerful reincarnated elder, whose power must be protected. Although some women in the native-oriented group do not isolate themselves during menstruation today, they are extremely careful during this period to refrain from contaminating others. An example is given in the quotations at the beginning of the chapter, in which a White woman fed a baby while she was menstruating and the baby died. The informant said of her child: "He had some little power, maybe from his grandfather. . . . You're not supposed to kiss a baby or anything then [while menstruating] and have to keep soiled things away from men's clothes and always keep clean. I never had any soiled things laying around." While she believed that her baby's death was due to the contact with the White woman, there was no personal blame, as the woman was ignorant of the taboo. The Menomini woman said, "I wasn't really blaming her. I was thinking the little boy had some power that was killed by her."

If . . . a man, fitted by his supernatural guardian with a tiny turtle, fish, or other small animal living in his vitals should eat food in . . . a dish . . . that had been touched by a menstruating woman, the tiny animal upon whose presence his good fortune depends will surely die and he will vomit it forth. The man may live after this; but his power is forever destroyed. [Skinner 1913:52]

In order to protect and maintain one's power, a person must at all times strive to be a proper Menomini. A good man respects the rights of others and does not arouse antagonism (particularly in older persons), lives quietly, observes the sacrifices required to maintain good relations with the sources of his powers, and is modest, even-tempered, and guards himself against undue pride. The necessary behaviors required of a good Menomini are incorporated into the Commandments of the Dream Dance Drum (*kaki·hkotakan te·we·hekan*). One of the owners of a Dream Dance drum relates some of these requirements:

They told us that when we talk about one person, you talk about God [*Ke·se·maneto·w*]. . . . Another thing. Everything God owns; He puts everything here. Indian should ask Him first; like if he should pick them berries or hunting deer, or anything like that. That's the way it should be done.

And the women, it's the same thing, should help one another. Like if one of them has a lot of work to do, the other women should make up their mind to help each other. Like sometimes a woman has got to scrub and clean up the house there, has too many kids, and couldn't do that.

All the members should be one person and treat each other right, just like sisters and brothers.

If someone owns something better than the other one, we should not be jealous just because he owns some good things. [Slotkin 1957:42–43]

One's power may also be strengthened by participating in a War Dance or by sponsoring ghost feasts for the deceased. During our period of study a ghost feast was held for a member of the group who was accidentally killed. The sister of the deceased was asked what the dead girl especially liked to eat, and these items were purchased—oranges, lemons for lemonade, peach halves, apples, sweet rolls. Her spirit was considered to be present.

If a person's power came from a spirit in the underworld, he or she is obligated to observe proper ritualistic behavior as those receiving other spirits do. Evil powers may also be inherited when an elder leaves a bag to a person. The bag must be "fed" by killing persons, often relatives. The witch takes the guise of an animal—dog, turkey, owl, bear, ball of fire, and the like—when he or she goes out to perform rituals. If the witch is killed while in animal form, it will return to its own form and then die in a few days. Sister Inez Hilger, in 1936, had an informant who inherited witch bags from a great grandmother and used one as she had seen her grandmother do:

I inherited her two "medicine bags"—the very powerful one, and another one. I no longer have them. Having them in my possession put me under an obligation to kill one person each year with each bag. This is our old belief. But I did not wish to kill persons. I knew I would regret such a thing on my deathbed. I gave the two bags to two old, distant relatives. I had kept the bags stored in a trunk for a long time. I did use one of them once in the manner in which I had seen my great-grandmother use it. And this is how I used it: I attached a strap to the bag, slipped the strap over my head so it rested on my right shoulder, slipped my left arm through, and let the bag rest on my abdomen just in front of the left hip bone. The body had to be nude when this "medicine bag" was being used, for the bag had to rest on the bare skin. I talked to the bag and then slipped into bed. When in bed I changed into an animal that I wanted to be changed into. I changed into a dog. That is, my spirit changed into a dog; my body stayed in bed. Then I went out of my body but I did not go far away. I only went out here into the woods, and up this hill and then I returned to my body. I did no harm to anyone. If anybody had touched me while in this spirit form, I would have been able to return to my body, but I would have died soon after that. [Hilger 1960:56]

Contemporary Menomini informants in the native-oriented group have the same patterned set of beliefs concerning witches as those described by Skinner in 1913. Concerning the bag, one informant remarked:

He [father] said that when a person gits that bag, he's supposed to use it on somebody and if he doesn't, one of his own dies. ["Feeding the Bag," in L. Spindler 1970]

Another informant describes the witch transformed into a ball of light:

You can see them [witches] coming in a big cloud of light, and you have to watch out. The person gets scairt like he was hypnotized. When this young woman's baby died [next door] they watched around the house and graveyard but couldn't see it [the witch]. It was slick work that time. [L. Spindler, field notes]

A different informant describes the witch transformed into a dog:

My dad started to get witched one time. Dr. White gave him up as dead. That night some boys was goin' to Neopit and met a dog. That dog looked

at them and up to his whiskers it was all fire in there and they killed the
dog and my dad started gettin' better the next day and we heard an old lady
died in S. Branch and so we knew she did it. [L. Spindler, field notes]

The people quoted above are all women. It became obvious after several
periods of field work that Menomini native-oriented males talked about witchcraft
reluctantly, as it was too dangerous. Transitional males spoke somewhat more
freely on the subject, but the acculturated and elite males didn't speak of it at
all. A partial explanation for this discrepancy in response between males and
females could be that the women in this male-oriented culture recognize their
lesser involvement with the important male-dominated "instrumental" activities
of the culture, related to the maintenance of the society's institutions. Therefore,
their "expressive" roles of mother and wife (see Zelditch 1955 for instrumental-
expressive differentiation) may free them somewhat from direct responsibility
for the consequences of dealing with important areas such as those subsumed
by the "supernatural." A reinforcing factor may have been the fact that the
anthropologist collecting the responses is also a woman from a society where
the men have played the important instrumental roles.

*Witches and wizards are persons who, through self-mortification, such as
fasting and sacrifices, have obtained the patronage of some one of the Evil
Powers, in return for which they are obliged to slay members of their own
tribe as votive offerings. They attack and destroy their victims by magically
transforming themselves into balls of fire, owls, bears, foxes, turkeys, and other
animals, and traveling from great distances at night with remarkable speed.
Arrived at the lodge of his prey, the sorcerer discharges enchanted arrows at
him, causing disease, and, if the attacks are repeated, death. Witches are known
to have magic bundles, the most notorious of which contain the entire hide of
a bear, or the skin of a horned owl, which are worn when assuming the shapes
of these animals. With the skins is included a bandoleer, or shoulder pouch,
covered with tiny bags holding bad medicines, the worst of which are portions
of the body of the terrible Horned Hairy Snake.
The witches are said to be associated in a society having eight members,
four using the bear and four the owl as mediums of murder. Their rites are
said to include a disgusting form of cannibalism, for witches are supposed to
haunt the graveyards where their victims are buried, and so magically to
obtain the heart and lungs of the murdered persons, which they are credited
with devouring. Witches also destroy their victims by shooting and stabbing
rude effigies of them made on the ground or on birch-bark, or by torturing dolls
of grass or wood. They also steal the luck away from hunters, sending their
arrows or bullets astray; they cause children to drown; and practice other
nefarious arts.* [Skinner 1921:69–71]

One pervasive theme in Menomini tales and myths is that the hero is
helpless without his particular dream-bestowed power, and that he may lose it
by abuse, neglect, or lack of constraint. If his bundle is lost or stolen, he is easily
overcome by his enemies, or he may starve because he can kill no game. However,

the hero is particularly successful only because he has acquired a certain power. Similarly, in contests between individuals, such as those in a struggle between a great *mete·w* and a *wa·beno*, one of the central figures realizes and admits that his power is not strong enough to withstand that of the other, so gives in without further contest. The individual is dependent upon this power as something not of himself, but as something gained by him through the exercise of proper behavior, of which general constraint is an important aspect. (Skinner and Satterlee, part 3, 1915; Hoffman 1896; Bloomfield 1928.)

Whether it is power from good spirits of the upper world, or evil spirits of the underworld, the importance of gaining and maintaining power remains today at the core of the entire native-oriented Menomini value system. One's power—measured in terms of one's ability to conquer the environment—may fluctuate, but it is vital to one's existence. All persons in the group must continually attempt to appease the power-giving spirits.

CEREMONIAL ORGANIZATIONS AS RELATED TO POWER

The *Mete·wen*

The Menomini traditionally had a number of specialized rites. The most important was the *mete·wen* (Mystic Rite or Medicine Dance). Today the *ni·mihe·twan* (Dream Dance) is the important rite for the native-oriented Menomini and is held most often. As one Menomini remarked:

I think the *mete·wen* is just going to go away gradually; that's what I think. There isn't enough people interested in it, the younger folks . . . they only had *mete·wen* once a year, and that isn't enough for anybody to learn anything from it. And that's what I think; maybe they [the elders] are not interested in it, they don't have it often enough. [Slotkin 1957:13]

This seems to be a rather accurate assessment of what is happening. The Medicine Dance is of less importance today than it was only a few years ago. The four-day ritual is so complicated that only a few of the elders know it in its entirety, and most of them are very aged. The authors were fortunate enough to witness three Medicine Dances during their period of fieldwork.

The Medicine Dance and the Dream Dance are both rituals directly related to the Menomini concept of power—power to combat evil, power to use evil at times, and power to control the environment. The stated intent of the Medicine Dance ritual is to prolong life and insure the good health of its members by assisting them in gaining access to power and protecting them against the machinations of witches and evil power.

The *mete·wen* is the older of the two ceremonies and has the most elaborate ritual. Most students agree that it is probably of early postcontact origin and, as Keesing (1939:47) suggests, possibly a phenomenon springing from the same source of insecurity created by the first impact of contact with Western civilization as in other "nativistic" movements. Many of the elements, however, are of great antiquity, and the ritual and beliefs of the Lodge have been a funda-

The mete·wen *shelter, 1954. The wall tents on the sides are occupied by onlookers and relatives who are not in the society.*

The initiates sit quietly and solemnly, waiting for the ritual to begin.

mental aspect of the religious systems of all central Algonkians. This organization still played a vital role in the lives of the native-oriented Menomini until as late as 1960 and remains an integral part of the belief system of the native oriented.

The *mete·wen* is an exclusive organization with membership by invitation or inheritance of a medicine bag. The candidate pays for his or her instructions in installments. An installment is made for each of the four parts of the ritual after the part has been repeated in instruction. It is believed that the teachings are of no use if the payments are not large. Each member becomes a possessor of a medicine bag (an otter, mink, or other whole small animal skin filled with small packets of herbal medicine), the power to shoot a small magically endowed cowrie shell (a *megi·s*), and a medicine for retrieving it.

The acknowledged intent of the society is to prolong human life, and to this end the lore of real herb, root, and magical medicines, as well as its special property, is zealously guarded. Every prescription is strictly proprietary. Even at the point of death a person may not have it without paying an exorbitant price, though he be a relative or a friend of the owner, and new discoveries and revelations are kept secret until purchased. The lodge also seeks, for a price, to see to the final settlement of the souls of the dead in their future abode, and the relatives pay well for ceremonies in behalf of the deceased. [Skinner 1920:22–23]

The Medicine Dance ritual, which was given to the Menomini by the culture hero Mɛʔnapos, is divided into four parts.

The ritual of the Menomini medicine lodge is divided into four parts, the first of which is the dramatization of the initiation of the hero-god Mä'näbus, the ceremonies representing the first mythical performance of the rites. The leaders impersonate the great Gods Below and Above the novice Mä'näbus. The second part is the Jebainoke {or Jebainoket}, the private funeral ceremony at which the soul of a deceased member is recalled from the hereafter, feasted, and dismissed forever, according to the command of Mä'näbus, the master. The third part is the Uswinauamikäsko, or Obliteration Ceremony, a public and more elaborate form of the Jebainoke held in a medicine lodge erected at or near the grave. [Skinner 1920:23–24]

One ceremony which we attended was an initiation ceremony for a young woman who was taking the place of her deceased father and a reinstatement or renewal ceremony for an old member. In conversation with the woman before the ceremony she said excitedly:

They're gonna have a dance here next week—Saturday night and all day Sunday and I'm gonna be put in to take over my dad's place. We're givin' a joint dance with J. His wife died about a year ago too. The old men are out cuttin' poles for the lodge now. My sister said to be sure and invite you folks. It's kinda easier givin' it together; all the food and presents ain't so much then.

[Do you know what the different motions and songs mean in the dance?]
I don't know much about it. I've watched it. [She feigns innocence, as the ceremony is secret.] They haven't told me. They're gonna sing evenings at L.'s and they'll tell me then what to do. F. is supposed to tell me all about it.
[Where will you get your medicine bag?]
They're havin' trouble about that. I don't know what become of it [father's medicine bag]. They're tryin' to get a bag from someone who has three or four. They'd have to clean the bag out. Each person would donate a little medicine for my bag. F. [medicine man] will tell me all about it.
[Who will take your father's place?]
There'll be some Winnebago, M., who is gonna take the place of my father

While the metɛˑwen *drum is beaten and one of the elders sings, a ritual offering of water is made to the candidate.*

Saturday night and after that he's like my dad. They're gonna "dress him" and adopt him Saturday night and give him a new suit of clothes and a rug and feed him. There'll be people from Wabeno and Wisconsin Rapids there.

It can be inferred that the length of time spent in learning the ritual and the amount of payment is greatly reduced today.

The singing for these particular Medicine Lodge rites began three days before the opening of the formal ceremony. Three elders talked to the deceased man's "spirit" just "like he was here," to inform him that a *metɛwen* was being held for him and to ask him if the gifts were sufficient, and if it was alright for M. to take his place as a stepfather for the two initiates, and other of the deceased relations.

The sponsor was a Catholic who said, "I wish I had followed that up, but I was baptized too soon." He owns an inherited medicine bag and feels that his wife died because the bag's "hunger" had not been satisfied by the giving of a ceremony. So he proposed that one be given so that "no more bad luck" would befall any members of his family.

No medicine bag for the initiate was available. "A week ago the hock shop [in Shawano] was full of them," said one of the women charged with responsibility by the sponsor for arrangements, "but everybody must of got theirs for the dance, so there's none left when we need one." George Spindler, commissioned as one of the four *skaˑpeˑwes* (ritual attendants and messengers) for the affair, was given two wool blankets and two packages of plug tobacco and asked to approach several elders who were thought to have bags, but who, for various reasons, were not coming to the ceremony. These attempts were unsuccessful, and the ceremony began without any bag for the initiate. The problem was solved when one of the Winnebago visitors gave up an "extra one" she had in exchange for the blankets and tobacco.

One of the high points of the ceremony was the "dressing" of the visitor taking the initiate's father's (recently deceased) place as ritual father. Behind a blanket held up by two of the *ska·pɛ·wes* he was washed and then dressed from the skin out, with necktie, tie clasp, socks, shoes, underwear, suit, and hat. After that, with the blanket down, he was fed a complete meal, with soup, fried chicken, potatoes, rice, blueberry pie, and coffee, which he ate on an oilcloth spread out before him, in his new clothing. Finished with his meal, which he ate slowly and thoroughly while everyone watched, he led each of four dancing rounds, carrying one of the blankets given to him, and a new aluminum pail.

The Medicine Lodge ceremony just referred to was held in a long, round-roofed structure with rounded ends made of bent saplings and covered with canvas instead of the bark that was used in earlier days. The lodge was approximately 50 feet long and 15 feet wide. Within it was an elongated circular path around which the members danced, with a hearth at one end and a mat for the candidate to kneel on (or fall on) at the other. On a cross-pole in the middle hung the blankets and calico that were to be given by the families "putting up" the ceremony to the four leaders after the ritual was finished. On another

The ritual father dances around the lodge with some of his gifts.

mat along one side the leaders sat, giving their chants, telling the legends, or beating the water drum. Along the horizontal poles of the framework of the sides hung the medicine bags of the members, when they were not being used. The ritual continued from sunset one day to sunset the next. The four *ose·ha·wuk* (*metɛ·wen* leaders), sometimes singly, sometimes together, exhorted the members to follow the *metɛ·wen* way carefully and told the story of the Lodge's origin, interspersing their telling with songs that can be sung correctly only by a throat long practiced in giving the right resonance and tremolo to what seem to be minor keys. At intervals some, or all, of the members danced around the circular path with a loose-jointed step that was at the same time graceful and bearlike, holding their medicine bags before them with both hands, and shaking them at the nondancers so that they might feel their power. Occasionally, the peculiar cry that is the earmark of the *metɛ·wen* ceremony, "Whe-ho-ho-ho-ho!" rang out above the reverberations of the water drum.

The most dramatic part of the ritual was the time when the candidate was "shot" with the medicine bags of the four *ose·ha·wuk*, and then received her own, to become a fullfledged *metɛ·w*. Before this important moment, the candidate had received instructions from one of the *ose·ha·wuk* concerning the use of the medicine bag and the powerful medicines it contained. She had to pay for these revelations. She passed through many hours of ritual leading up to this point, for the "shooting" does not take place until a few hours before the close of the ceremony.

The candidate dances slowly around the lodge with one of the elders behind her.

The candidate collapses when "shot"; the old man with her was reinitiated in this ceremony.

When the long-awaited moment arrived, the male members of the Lodge danced around the long circle of the lodge, chanting as they went, to the accompaniment of water drum and rattle. The four leaders passed the candidate, then proceeded to the end of the lodge opposite the candidate, who was standing before a blanket spread on the ground. At this point one of the leaders chanted, "I will now shoot the *megi·s* [the cowrie shell] at her, that she may feel its power and become our child." Then, one at a time, each of the *ose·ha·wuk* blew on his medicine bag, and danced rapidly toward the candidate, shouting, "Whe-ho-ho-ho-ho-ho!" When he neared the candidate, who was trembling in anticipation of receiving the full impact of the powerful medicines, he jerked his medicine bag up and forward, at the same moment crying "Ho!" and thrusting it directly at the initiate. The candidate shuddered with the force of the shot. She was not making believe, for she had been taught that the medicine bag has great power, and she felt it, as one man expressed it, "Just like lightning had struck you."

When the last of the four *ose·ha·wuk* had shot her with his medicine bag, the power-filled candidate collapsed, apparently knocked unconscious by the terrible force. She appeared to remain unconscious until she was revived. While one of the leaders chanted, "Here you have seen the power of the *metε·wen* and the *megi·s* given to *Mε?napos* by *Mε·c-awε·tok* [the Supreme Being] that we have gotten from him. Our sister lying before us has had it put into her heart. She, and all of our children will feel its strength." The other *metε·wuk* then gathered around the prostrate form and covered her with their medicine bags. Then an *ose·ha·w* raised the initiate by her shoulders, shook her, and a *megi·s* fell from her mouth. As consciousness returned to the initiate, she slowly rose from the ground and began a dance, imitating the Great Bear, while showing her *megi·s* to all around her. Then she went before the *ose·ha·wuk*; one of whom lectured to her about the meaning of her initiation and presented her with his own medicine bag. The initiate has to try to see if she has the sacred power. She blew on the bag, then circled the lodge, dancing slowly and thrusting the bag at various of the members. As each *mete·w* was shot, he sank to the ground, but revived quickly, got up, and circled the lodge himself, using his own medicine bag in the same way.

This is a dangerous time for anyone not a member of the lodge to be too close, for he may get hit with a stray shot. If this does happen, everything stops, while the *ose·ha·wuk* seek out the careless *mete·w* who aimed so badly, and shoot him in turn. This, along with a number of other procedures, usually enables the leaders to extract the stray *megi·s*, and the victim survives.[12]

By this time it was noon of the last day of the ceremony. It continued until sundown, with more chants, drumming, shooting, and ritual. However, for the initiate the climax was over, for she had new life and power. She had become a *mete·w*.

> *Now comes the most spectacular, and one of the most important, parts of the ceremony—the shooting of the sacred power into the candidate by the four osehauwuk. Lining up in the eastern end of the lodge, each shaman in turn takes his animal skin medicine-bag, blows on its head, and holding it before his breast, trots down the lodge. In front of the candidate he points it, jerks its head forward, and the essence of its power passes into the candidate's body. The novice quivers, and, on the fourth shot, collapses, falling on his face. The fourth shaman leaves his medicine-bag lying on the candidate's back, for him to keep as his own thereafter. The shamans then shake the candidate to remove all the beads from his body.* [Skinner 1920:179–180]

The leaders of the *mete·wen* are all-important, for it is only from their memories that the secret songs, speeches, and steps of the ritual may issue. There were only four such men during the authors' fieldwork period who knew the ritual, which accounts in large measure for its dying out. Only one of these four men is still alive (1970). The Lodge is probably only about 300 years old, as suggested earlier, but many of the native-oriented Menomini today think of it as being the "real" Menomini religion.

The medicine bags have both good and evil power. Though they are all-important in the life-renewal aspects of the *mete·wen* and contains herbs and medications for curing, they are called "witch bags" in English by members and nonmembers alike. Everyone agrees that the bags can kill, and that a bag unsatiated by a ceremony becomes very dangerous, causing death or illness for the owner or his close kin.

---

[12] George Spindler was hit by a stray shot and spent a week in the hospital with a fever of "undiagnosed origin." This was interpreted as proof of the power of the "medicine." (See G. Spindler and L. Spindler 1970.)

Your grandfathers give you in addition all sorts of medicine-bags that shall be right and great for you and your people to use. The greatest one, to begin with, is the otter-skin; it is the leader. Next is the mink, especially a white one, if you can get it, after the fashion of your grandfathers' bags. Different kinds of animals you shall use in their likeness, and it shall continue in rotation along the north side {of the lodge}.

The serpent-skin, representing the horned, hairy snakes, shall be the bag of those who know and have that one and its medicines of both good and evil. [Skinner 1920:61–62]

The *Ni·mihɛ·twan*

The *ni·mihɛ·twan* or Dream Dance,[13] introduced about 1879, is today the major ceremonial organization still operating among the native-oriented Menomini. It too, like the *metɛ·wen*, originated as a "nativistic" movement—a reaction to the disorganizing and threatening impact of Western civilization. It is related to the "Ghost Dance" originating farther west but is more accomodative in orientation. The rite represents a combination of some Christian with many aboriginal elements, but is essentially native North American in pattern and has been invested with characteristic Menomini attitudes and values.

Unlike the *metɛ·wen*, membership in the Dream Dance group is relatively open, and the sacred knowledge is obtained at the cost of only a few ritual gifts. Further, the weekly meetings or seasonal rites are more intimate and more directly related to everyday life. Since the rite is definitely a product of acculturative pressures, it is flexible and has subsumed many of the functions of other rites. The dogma and cosmology of the organization resemble traditional Menomini beliefs. It is crucial that a man obtain the supernatural power necessary to enable him to carry out his activites, and, as was true before the Dream Dance came to the Menomini, this is done by petitioning the spirits, but through the sacred drum and the ritual related to it.

The doctrines of the Dream Dance group are based on revelations received by a young Sioux woman from the Great Spirit. He gave her the original Drum and taught her the rituals. One of the members related the contemporary version of the origin myth:

They who are White [White soldiers] killed almost all the Sioux [in a battle]. It was then that the woman—she is said to have hidden among reeds; in order to breathe there, she parted the leaves [of the reeds]. She probably lay in the water for four days. When four days had passed, it is said that the Spirit [awɛ·tok] then came to her. He probably told her, "Come, arise." At that time she thought it was only some person; she did not know that it was the Spirit who was speaking to her. And he told her this. A little while later she arose from the water. Oh, I pity you!" he told her. "Arise!" he told her. "You will go eat; it is I who will take you. Nothing is going to happen to

---

[13] *Ni·mihɛ·twan* means literally "dancing rite," but it has long been referred to as the Dream Dance.

you; it is I who pity you," that one probably told her, he who was standing there above the water. . . . Then he is said to have taken her where these White men [*mo·hkoma·nak*] were eating; he took her there. "No one will see you. It is I who intend to help you," he told her. "Do not be afraid; come with me." Then she went with that one; he took her there. A big table was there [in the White soldiers' camp]; one plate was not being used. It is said that he then pointed it out to her, so that she could eat as much as she desired [invisible to the White soldiers]. When she was full, he took her some place.

She went with him. When she opened her eyes, she saw that Drum there. "Well, then, this is what I give you," he told her. At that time the Drum probably made a noise, and she saw the drumsticks moving. She heard singing. She listened to them there; at first she heard them singing four songs there.

Well, after this was finished, the Spirit spoke to her. He told her everything; he told her how the Indian should perform it [the Dancing Rite]; he gave her to understand how to do everything that is good. [He told her] the way everyone should act: to help himself, to be good to one another. That they should not be the way they still are—people harming one another, killing one another—no! That was what the Spirit told her. "I give you only that which is good," he told her. [Translation, in Slotkin 1957:17–18.]

Many years ago, during a war between the Indians and the Whites, the natives were driven out of their country. A young girl became separated from the rest of her party and secreted herself in the bushes until dark, when she made her way to a river and hid under an overhanging bank. There she remained for eight days. All that time she had nothing to eat and saw no one.

As she fasted with a downcast heart, a spirit came to her in her hiding place, and called to her in her own language: "Poor little girl. Come out and eat. It is time for you to break your fast. Do not be afraid, I am going to give you happiness because your people have been expelled from their country, and because of your suffering you have won my pity. Now your troubles are at an end. Go and join the enemy, but say nothing. Go to their table, help yourself, and no one shall see that you are not one of them. Then come away and you shall find your friends. You shall travel through the thick forests and over open plains, even among the White people, but fear nothing. Look straight ahead and not backwards or downwards. Even though the White people pass so closely in front of you as almost to touch you, do not fear, for they shall not see you."

"When you arrive among your people once more, eat and be satisfied. Then you may all escape through the prairies and the woods, through the ranks of the enemy, and you shall never be seen, for I shall protect you. When they have all reached safety I want you to tell them that I sent you to give them power and strength. Instruct them to make a little drum {the drum has grown bigger since} to decorate it, and elevate it above the ground, for as it came from the heavens, so it must stay above the earth. Then your people are to beat upon it whenever you desire my aid; and, as your prayers arise to my ears with the sound of the drum, I shall grant your heart's desire."

The Dream Dance drum most frequently used in services. The beadwork around the top tells the story of the origin of the rite. Note also the ordinary drumsticks, sacred pipe, tobacco, and the "chief" drumstick (beaded, to the left of the drum).

"When you feel sad at heart, or sick, or fear war, or desire victory in battle, tell it to the drum, which you shall call your grandfather, and give it a present of tobacco, and your words shall be wafted to me. You shall receive help every time you use it, but you must not beat upon it without cause. You shall have joy and success in all your undertakings. Tobacco must be used to make the spirit of the drum, your grandfather, happy, and love and friendship shall rule among its users."

"No worthy man shall be prevented from taking part in these rites, and those who participate must live clean and honest lives, cease drinking, be sober, follow the rules I have laid down for you. . . . You must never neglect the drum, your grandfather, and you must use it at intervals in remembrance of me. Now, go where your people are, and tell them of my instructions, and cause them to spread the news throughout all the Indian nations, that they too may receive my help." [Skinner 1915:175–176]

The *ni·mihe·twan* ritual centers upon a large drum, about 30 inches in diameter, about 12 inches deep, constructed of rawhide stretched over a circular wooden frame. There are four such drums in the native-oriented group. The head of the drum is painted red, to symbolize the dangerous spirits, and blue, to symbolize the good spirits—corresponding to the dualistic concept of the universe held traditionally by the Menomini—with a yellow line bisecting these two colors to symbolize the course of the sun and the right path of life. The sides are decorated with beadwork in the form of symbols denoting the origin of the rite.

Each drum has a number of offices, which are related to each "leg" of the drum—one for each of the four directions of the compass. There is a drum owner, a man in the older age group, who retains major responsibility for the conduct of the ceremonies in which it is used. He is the authority on proper ritual, and he is supposed to look out "like a father" for the people occupying offices connected with his drum and their families. "He sits there just like God, and watches what we do. If we do anything wrong [in the ritual] he is supposed to tell us. He is supposed to look out for us too, and not be stingy with anything." There is also a "keeper" for each drum who maintains the drum in his home in its sacred wrappings, keeps a lighted lantern near it at night, and is responsible for its care.

When a "song service" (which may be held any time) or a seasonal rite is being conducted, from four to eight men sit around the drum, singing in chorus and hitting the drum in unison. The drum has a deep and resonant tone that is exhilarating, if deafening—especially in the confines of a small room. The floor, windows, and human bodies vibrate with every beat. The people claim that the service makes them "feel good," that they forget their worries and troubles. The ritual is, indeed, a means of renewing power. "The old man in the drum," *Kemɛ·hsomen*, is the intermediary between man and spirits, particularly *Kesɛ·maneto·w* (Great Spirit). When the drum is hit, its voice, symbolized by a

Children at the Zoar community hall, where most Dream Dance song services were held.

small bell suspended on a wire inside the drum and most apparent in the deep voice of the drum itself, notifies the spirits through *Kemε·hsomen* that the ceremony is being held and asks for their "blessings." "When that drum is hit, his [*Kemε·hsomen's*] voice is sent all over, in all four directions, to all those spirits. *Kesε·maneto·w* hears that and gives us what we ask for. That old man in the drum gets those messages out." It is believed that in order to keep group and individual access to sacred, life-giving power intact, it is necessary to hold the seasonal rites and frequent song services. Without this access to power, bad luck will ensue. Through the medium of the rites and proper ceremonial sacrifices (mostly of tobacco), the drums are a means of renewing power and therefore securing good luck, as well as revitalizing the spirits of the participants.

During the meetings, when drumming, singing, or praying is not going on, someone is speaking. One of the old men exhorts all present to do the right things, usually ending with a plea to observe more closely the old ways. The drum has a number of special commandments (*kaki·hkotakan tε·wε·hekan*) that are supposed to guide the conduct of the men and women who are members of the Dream Dance group. The requirements are congruent with those accepted for being a "good" Menomini (see specific requirements given in the section on maintaining power, p. 51). After the meetings anyone may speak. All these speeches are presented and received in a highly formal and very serious manner. Anyone who gets up to speak, including even the missionary, is heard with the greatest courtesy and respect. Sometimes during the meeting, usually at the beginning or end of any speech in which exhortation or explanation is involved, the speaker says something like this: "I am not proud just because I know this little. It is because my father was important in this and I got it from him, not because of myself" (see p. 20).

The drum (*tε·wε·hekan*) is the most sacred object in the Dream Dance or powwow for a variety of reasons. It is the most important material embodiment of power. It is believed that the Great Spirit, and all the good spirits he created, put some of their power into the original Drum given to the Sioux woman who is believed to have introduced the ritual to the Menomini (Slotkin 1957:35). When asked what the Drum's power can do, one informant replied:

> Well, if you ask him anything, if you want something, put your tobacco there. Say, "I want to go hunting; I want to go hunt deer. I want to go pick berries." Anything like that. Put your tobacco in there. Not all persons can do that successfully; just those that believes in the Drum, he can get help from the Drum. [Slotkin 1957:35]

It is believed that the power of the drum is so strong that the drum, like the Menomini elder performing an act of witchcraft, can cause some misfortune to come to a person who openly flouts the moral code of the group. An elderly informant relates an incident of this sort:

> Some way, this old lady got mad, and took an axe, a sharp axe, and hit the Drum. She was going to bust that Drum entirely. [She] hit that Drum once;

The elders watch over the Dream Dance services.

couldn't break it. And hit that Drum again twice; couldn't do nothing. So she hits that Drum again third time; no. But the fourth time, then that axe went through. [What does that show?] That shows that there's something in the Drum, pretty strong. When she bust that Drum [on] purpose—that old lady had a brother—and she lost this brother right away, because she done this wrong. [Slotkin 1957:36]

The drums are also a source of individual powers, particularly for the drum keeper who has the drum in his house, and cares for it. The relationship is virtually identical to that maintained with the guardian spirit gained through the Great Fast, usually through the medium of a sacred bundle representing that spirit, and with the relationship now maintained with individual, inherited guardians. One night a drum keeper had a dream. In the dream he was out hunting and two deer approached him. One of them said, "I thought I'd tell you, that fellow [the other deer], he just gave you his life." This dream prompted the man to go out hunting the next evening. In order to insure the prophecy and to take advantage of the offer of the deer to "give up his life," the Menomini man made a sacrifice to the drum in order to notify the powers of his and the deer's decision, and to secure the "luck" (the power) to perform the deed successfully. He said:

Well, I had some tobacco, and I cut it up and put it in the tobacco boxes [ceremonial wooden bowls associated with the drum] and lit some of it in two pipes. Anything you do, you got to have tobacco. Just the plug kind—it goes farther that way. If you're going out hunting, if you're keeping a drum, and you have some tobacco cut up in fine pieces, you put it by the drums, and you smoke some yourself. I smoked first one [pipe] then the other. And I talked to that drum, like if I was talking to you. I'd say. "I'm going out. I'm going to try to get some meat. Would you mind helping me out?"

He went out hunting after the sacrifice to the drum. He waited by a salt lick for several hours until it was almost too dark to see any more. Finally, two deer approach the lick. One of them threw up his head, startled, probably, by the scent of the man, and bounded off in the brush. The other started to run, then stopped and turned toward the man. The Menomini shot this one, the one that gave him his life in the dream the night before, through the heart. "That's happened many times. I'd ask for help. . . . I'd get it. I believe to this day that it's this way. I asked for that deer, and I got it."

The native-oriented system of belief is encapsulated in this sequence of events just described: the dependence of the individual upon revelation through dreams; the importance of keeping one's access to power intact; the dependence upon the power thus gained for success in all the ventures of life; the quiescent, waiting expectancy that if the proper rituals are observed, "fate" (as we might term it) will provide; the autonomous character of the relationship between these powers and the individual; all of this is clear. The Dream Dance reaffirms the validity of the traditional cultural system each time it is held, even though it began as a religious movement in recent times. Without such visible manifestations of a separate identity and belief, the native-oriented group is unlikely to exist for long.

Membership in the Dream Dance is dwindling today. One member sadly stated: ". . . we ain't much of us left. . . . And we are short handed today. We ain't got enough people to fill out the Drum the way it's supposed to be" (Slotkin 1957:16). An elderly woman member of the group, when asked about the fate of the group, passionately exclaimed:

. . . they say, "It's going to be lost, after a while." The different Catholic people, they always say, "It's going to be lost, this Indian way." No! She [is] not going [to be] lost! There's lots of Indians all over, all kinds; the same religion what I got, he's got it! She's not going [to be] lost! If every tribe said that, she'd be lost; she'd be lost, I guess. But never! She's not going [to be] lost! I know it myself! Lots [of people] know it! [Slotkin 1957:15]

The Okeceta·we·se·man

The Okeceta·we·se·man (Chief's, or Warrior's, Dance) is the third rite held by the native-oriented group. The Menomini had it "long ago." As one of the leaders explained:

It was a real War Dance then. They could take out the boys, and come back with the things they were after [scalps] before you [Whitemen] come over. It died out until just lately—it was lost. Then the Chippewa came over [about

1925] when I was a boy, and they told the Menomini, "We didn't come here to show you anything, but if you want to do it this way—you got some songs of your own, but maybe you'd like to do it the way we do it." So now this is a copy of the Chippewa, on the good side of it, not just for war. We use this now for a religion. Like if you were to go to church. Of course it's also used for the boys being drafted. We had a War Dance for the boys over there in Korea. We do it regularly for those boys.

The *okeceta·we·se·man* should be given with the seasonal rites of the *ni·mihe·twan*. "We always used to wind up the last day of the powwow with the War Dance. Now there's too many workin' so we let that last day go" (so the *ni·mihe·twan* can be held over the weekend). The War Dance, like the *ni·mihe·twan*, is often given more casually. The same leader continues:

We go over there . . . put tobacco down and just sing most every evening. Pretty soon the whole family was there. Then the neighbors would come over. It made a pretty good habit. It's the same way like with the *ni·mihe·twan*. You don't have to do it any certain date. There's regular ceremonies come just certain times of the year [seasonal rites] but otherwise it's any time you feel like it.

There are actually more War Dance drums in the native-oriented group than *ni·mihe·twan* drums. During our earlier field work there were at least six active drums, owned by specific individuals who were responsible for their care and use. The drums are not as sacred as those in the *ni·mihe·twan*, but no ceremonial object can be treated lightly. The War Dance is also more light-hearted than the *ni·mihe·twan*. At every rite we attended there was a lot of whooping and dancing, and the songs and drumming have a beat that is irresistible. Old men and women who appear to be on their last legs will get up during a dance and join in like they had suddenly lost their years. Nevertheless, there is a strong sacred aspect to the ceremony. Each of the songs is connected to the spirits in one of the four cardinal directions. When these songs are sung, these spirits are propitiated. Before the singing begins, a prayer of notification is given by one of the older men present who informs *ma?maw ko·hne·waw* (our Great Father), and the *awe·tokak* (spirits) of the purpose of the dance, and asks, for example, ". . . to help out each and every one in the hall at the time, and to watch out for those boys over in Korea."

When we recorded the songs at one rite, the leader asked, ". . . don't think anything of what this Whiteman is doing. It isn't as if we were doing anything wrong. Don't think hard about us, for what we are going to do." Near the end of the singing and dancing he named four songs, one for each cardinal direction, and said again to our Great Father:

I just named these four songs. For my part, I'm glad we did just what we did [recording the songs]. It was the right thing to do, so our children and

The War Dance drums and singers at an informal "song service."

their children can hear these songs. We don't want to bother you [our Great Father] with this and that. Maybe you could watch out for us, and all the boys over there. Now we will quit for awhile, so I will name those four songs. [G. Spindler, field notes]

Like the *ni·mihɛ·twan*, the *okeceta·wɛ·se·man* gains and maintains power. In this way it is a significant support for the continuing validity of the native-oriented group and its culture. Power maintenance is an underlying assumption in the conduct of the ceremony and the prayers. With power one can ward off sorcery, and even physical damage. The following version of the origin story makes this clear.

There was a great Menomini chief, the greatest of all, a long time ago, around Sturgeon Bay. They had guns by that time though. This chief was always leading war parties, with maybe thirty or forty Menomini. One time they went to fight the Sioux, two hundred of them. They was up a hill. There was a Potowatomi chief there too, but he was not as great. The Menomini told the Potowatomi chief to take the warriors back across the river. Then they, the Sioux, shoot at the Menomini chief alone. But they can't kill him. He run back and forth . . . they shoot, but they couldn't hurt him. So he come across the river and joined his [the Menomini war party]. Just then a last shot came across the river and hits him in the belly. Then he takes off his fur belt, strikes it, and bullets drop out, all flattened. That was how the *okeceta·wɛ·se·man* started, and they got all them songs in there. That chief, he had. that power.

He made that drum [the drum used in the rite] and he painted his totem on it. [G. Spindler, field notes]

WITCHCRAFT AND SOCIAL CONTROL

"No one has the right, on the basis of position or prestige, to exercise direct authority over another, not even a father over his son." This has been true of the Menomini since the time of the first contacts with Whites. In spite of certain formal structures of control during the pre-fur-trade period, it is probable that little direct secular authority was exercised by any leader among the Menomini. The Menomini were described by the Jesuit Father Allouez as a people who "have neither laws, nor police, nor magistrates to check disorder" (quoted in Keesing 1939:40). Even earlier Nicholas Perrote, the first French fur trader to visit the Menomini in 1667, remarked, "The savage does not know what it is to obey. . . . The father does not venture to exercise authority over his son. . . ." In 1913, Skinner, who worked closely with the Menomini for many years, remarked, "Among themselves, the rights of the individual were paramount. . . ." (Fuller versions of all these quotes are given in the introduction to this chapter.)

Among the present native-oriented group there is virtually no "leadership" in our sense of the word. One day a group was sitting about after an afternoon of dancing for tourists at a nearby "woodland bowl." It had been suggested that it would be helpful to have a battery-operated loudspeaker system for the master of ceremonies to use in his announcements to the assembled crowd. A Whiteman had offered to sell one to them for $50. The group was faced with the decision—should they or should they not buy it? Everyone sat quietly, saying nothing. A man of about forty years who was the intermediary between the group and the proprietors of the "bowl" and the owner of the loudspeaker system said, "What does the group think?" No one spoke for a long time. Someone finally said, "Well sometimes those people can't hardly hear." An indistinguishable murmur or two emitted from the assemblage—neither in agreement or dissent— or so it seemed, at least. Another period of quiet waiting. Another question by the intermediary. "Well, what does the group think?" Another murmur or two. So it went for some time. So long that the White man, who was waiting in his car for their decision, came over. "Well, what's the answer? Do you want to buy it or don't you? I can't wait all day." No response. In exasperation he stomped back to his car. "This man, he wants to know. What does the group think?" the query came again. No arguments, no open discussion, a few half-voiced murmurs. The people standing and sitting around left to attend to other business. Had a decision been reached? We thought not, but we were wrong. The intermediary went over to talk to the White man. He said, somewhat apologetically, "I guess the people don't want to spend the money." How did he know? Apparently, there had been no sentiments expressed in favor of the proposition other than the comment that "those people can't hardly hear." The absence of general consensus was enough. No "leader" would try to coerce or convince others that a given course of action was best, even though the intermediary thought, as we knew he did in this instance from other discussions with him, that a loudspeaker system was essential.

Elders are the "cynosure" of Menomini society—individuals who attract the bulk of attention and public prestige (see LaBarre 1946:173 for use of the term). Powers become stronger as one grows older. Thus the elders possess the greatest supernatural power because they have lived the longest, have knowledge of the esoteric rituals through which power is secured and maintained, and because, like children, they are closest to the supernatural. The Menomini regard life as a never-ending cycle through which one passes to be born again. This emphasis on age is patterned into the whole ceremonial and belief complex. It is the "old man" (grandfather) who is represented by the Dream Dance drum and who notifies the spirits related to the four directions of the needs and wants of the members. It is the old men who exhort the Medicine Lodge and Dream Dance groups to live right—not to be aggressive, not to boast, nor to gossip—to be generous and kindly to others, especially old people.

It is the elders who know the rituals, have the greatest access to the spirits and their powers, and, therefore, have potential for both beneficent and harmful behavior, can prophesy with their dreams, and are the authorities for questions on kin relationships. They are, therefore, all "leaders" in a sense. Their authority is sharply limited, however. Even the oldest man in the group referred to previously, the only member who went through the Great Fast, does not exert direct authority over others. For example, he once took some liberties with the Dream Dance drum of which he is "owner," kept by a younger man in his own home. To be a drum keeper is to be entirely responsible for the care and maintenance of the drum. Not even the owner is supposed to remove it to use in a ceremony without the direct knowledge and permission of the keeper. Under the pressure of unusual circumstances that arose in the absence of the drum keeper the old man removed the drum from the keeper's house to use in a ceremony. Upon learning of this, the younger man was quite disturbed and made a few very indirectly critical statements to others concerning the old man's action. At a song service some time later the old man arose to make a short speech. "My children, I am good to you. I care for you all the time. I pray for you to the Great Spirit. . . . Now somebody here does not feel good about things somehow." (See p. 22 for the full quote). He then proceeded to apologize indirectly for his action and added, "I did not want to hurt anyone's feelings. . . ." Even with his high status as an authority on all things important in the traditional framework of the native-oriented group, and even with his great capacity for good or evil because of his access to great powers, he did not and could not exercise direct authority over another younger man charged with an inviolable responsibility. In his indirect apology, he exhibited his concern about possibly having given offense for seeming to have exercised an authority he did not have. Never during our fieldwork did we observe an exception to the mode of leadership described.

In a system of this kind social control must function in indirect and subtle ways. Some of the ways in which social controls are effected among the native-oriented Menomini are: by indirect gossip (the drum keeper said enough about the old man's "indiscretion" so that the old man was brought to make a virtual apology); by reward (the old man can cure the ill and intercede for the people with his powers); by dreams [many times people have dreams that are publicly interpreted as prophecies of dire results for drinking, desertion, and failing to keep up ritual observances (see p. 49)]; by witchcraft (the constant threat that socially deviant behavior will result in the use of sorcery by the injured party). This last means of social control—witchcraft—is the most dramatic and the most effective.

According to the Menomini belief system, all powerful elders are potential witches. Again, the emphasis is upon power, which is today, and was probably in precontact times, the most important force in the lives of the Menomini. From the earliest accounts one might conclude that powerful shamans existed who possessed both good and evil tutelary powers and that the same shaman who performed an act of witchcraft on his patient might also cure him of the effects of this act. The contemporary Menomini witch also plays a segmentalized role, utilizing good as well as evil powers obtained from specific tutelary spirits of the underworld or through the use of a witch bag inherited from relatives or friends. So the same person who adopted several orphaned boys and who is in general considered wise and generous could, upon occasion, use his evil powers. The Menomini belief system also equates the witch with the "protector," one who watches to see that members of the group do not get too far out of line, that they conform to the basic rules that represent the Menomini value system. As the informant already quoted said, "He [an elder observing a ritual] sits there just like God, and watches what we do. If we do anything wrong, he is supposed to tell us. He is supposed to look out for us too, and not be stingy with anything."

In contrast to the situation in the majority of cultures for which witch-craft is described in the literature, the Menomini witch is not the deviant, the antisocial person, or the one who neglects social obligations, or the agitator who is accused of witchcraft and scapegoated by the community. He or she belongs to the group with greatest power and prestige—the elders. Social control is achieved among the native-oriented group by the threat of witchcraft by power figures rather than through accusation of the witch by the community. These dynamics of social control are strikingly different from those found in many other cultural systems. In contrast to the Menomini belief, which defines the witch as a respected elder who controls the deviant, the majority of cultures described in the literature define the witch as the recipient of punishment, a symbol of evil—the deviant who represents all of the negative values of the culture (see Fitzgerald 1964). The Menomini system, which is lacking in super-ordinate controls in the ordinary political power sense, provides fertile ground for the development of witchcraft as a kind of control.[14]

----

[14] We do not intend our analysis of witchcraft and social control in the present native-oriented group as a model to be applied without modification to the traditional cultural system when it was intact. Though the general characterization of the Menomini, past and present, as lacking strong forms of direct secular authority holds good, it is also true that most of the secular machinery of political and social adjudication and control that did exist in aboriginal times has long since ceased to function. It is probable that, as a consequence, witchcraft is more important in the native-oriented group today than it was in the past, even though many of the specific patterns and the general style have remained in force for a long time.

Everyone knows that he or she must repress hostile emotions (control of overt aggression), practice self-control (equanimity under duress), show concern for others (generosity, hospitality), respect others' rights (autonomy), show respect for elders, and never behave in an aggressive manner (quarrel, be too successful at any endeavor, show off). Children are taught by the elders at a very early age what proper behavior is. The Dream Dance drum has its own set of commandments similar to the requisites mentioned here (see p. 51). The good man lives quietly (quiescently) and observes constantly the sacrifices required to maintain good relations with the sources of his powers (in a latescent manner).

The fear of witchcraft is more than a concern about a specific act or situation; it is converted into a state of generalized apprehension. The very young child has been taught to fear owls, representing an evil spirit of the underworld, and as he grows older, he has the feeling that he is being constantly watched. This fear is not operative at the explicit level only but has become internalized so that it is "conscience-like" in its effect, with guilt factors present (L. Spindler 1970).

What are the penalties for deviating? Following are some accounts of native-oriented persons who were witched or anticipated being witched for exceeding cultural norms or disregarding amenities.[15] The incidents deal with persons known and named by the informants. Most members of the group know and agree upon the reason why the victims were witched though no one person told of being witched himself or herself. Members of this group do not feel the need to elaborate about incidents that happened in the distant past or to unknown people, unlike informants from other acculturative groups (see L. Spindler 1970).[16] The accounts are abbreviated and are related in a simple, matter-of-fact manner. The power of the witch is accepted as a given factor.

Offending Elders

Account 1

Old Sh. was goin' to give away his bag. We took care of him when he was alone. My father used to tell us we were supposed to always help out old people and do all we can and never make a fuss, because some day you might come across some old person who might happen to have that bag. No person can ever get the best of you or hurt you if you have that bag. "Just tell that old person you don't want no pay—don't take it at first. Turn

---

[15] Accounts 4, 5, 8, 9, 10 and 11 were given by women who are transitional now but who were raised by native-oriented parents, and their stories conform to the native-oriented pattern.

[16] The number and types of witchcraft accounts vary sharply in the various acculturative groups. This became clear after a detailed motif analysis of the accounts was made by L. Walker (1966). Accounts of the native-oriented members involved only "basic Menomini" motifs (see L. Spindler 1970). The accounts of witchcraft at other levels include introduced elements foreign to the traditional pattern as well as elaborations of old elements.

it down so you won't hurt their feelings and make him think you did it just for pay."

Sh. thought a lot of me and said, to my husband, "Your wife will lead you right." One time Sh. said if we wanted it [the bag], no one could pick on us. He asked us and said that he was gonna leave it. He asked me one evenin', "What do you think? Would it be right for you to take that?"

Another thing they used to say if you hurt old men's feelings, your child might die and hurt your feelings. I talked to Sh. in a nice way and tried to find a way not to hurt his feelings.

Account 2

[Question: Did your mother or father do much preaching, telling you what you should do?]

Yes. My mother did a lot of preachin'. She always told me to be nice to people, especially older people. She said to always wait on older people and never ask them for anything or they might hurt you. When I married B. she said, "Always be good to that old lady [mother-in-law]. Beat her up in the morning and get breakfast and do what she says. Don't lie around and look at books or anything like that. Get up early and work real hard, then she won't get mad at you. If she does, she won't hurt you, but she'll get someone you like best like your brother or mother or sister."

Account 3

A long time ago they never took children to doin's. If they did, the child had to sit still, because if it would stare at one person, the person wouldn't like it. My mother never took us anyplace. It's different now. All those old people are gone. There was one old lady we was always afraid of. When they'd have a powwow down at the hall full of people, one old lady would just walk around and look at each person and size them up from head to foot. M. used to put her head down and she'd feel that old lady lookin' at her. When they had the Medicine Dance, that old lady used to shoot her bag [beaver skin] around. It's kinda dangerous you know. You still can't trust 'em [people shooting medicine bags during the mete·wen ceremony].

Account 4

[Did you hear much about witchcraft?]

Yes, one time when it happened to my sister's baby. N. [medicine man] helped me. My sister's girl was threatened by an old lady who said she would make her pay for not payin' more attention to her. The baby got scairt by a pine snake, like N. said it would. It was a big, fat, healthy baby too. The old lady that threatened her had a bag [a witch bag]. The baby got sick and we went to the hospital and they sent it back, as they couldn't find anythin' wrong. We gave her N.'s medicine but the baby died. Maybe that other person's medicine was more powerful. There are four [witches] in a clan. They all work together. There's a trail over here. My Grandmother hears them at night.

My baby was threatened and I went to N. for medicine. He knew who done it and gave me medicine so I could find out. With one dose I could hear when it went by. I'd hear it but I couldn't see. It was just somethin' that wasn't human. Usually they do that to you [witch you] because of jealousy. You never know the reason why they done it.

Account 5

Do you know a long time ago we didn't use to laugh in front of an old person? They was awful strict about that. They [the old person] might make your mouth turn [paralyzed].

Aggressive Behaviors

Account 6

If people used to dress better than the rest or think they were somebody, they had to watch out.

Account 7

I had a step brother who was killed like that. He used to be a *good cook*. He was a *good little hunter* too and just for that reason they witched him. There was one man that used to come and tell my mother she thought she was smart to have a boy like that, so she suspected him.

S. was witched because he was such a *good dancer*. He was only two or three years old. He had two good legs then and somebody didn't like it. His dad knew who did that. He couldn't do anythin'. [This same incident was related by other informants, see Account 9; the victim, now a grown man, was crippled.]

Account 8

[Question: Do you ever hear stories about witchcraft?]
I've heard lots.

Well, I'll tell you. My sister could speak English real good. She was a good piano player—graduated from Flandreau—a pretty girl about five feet three inches. When she came home she couldn't get no job in the office. Finally they put her on the advisory board but not much money. She was for the Zoar district. Some people at Zoar didn't like her—she was *too smart*. We were told someone witched her and she gradually failed and got sick and died. We knew who did it. My father said never to say anything. People will have to pay. One old man, C. D., said some kind of creature would howl around our house when my sister died. I went out in the evening to see. I would stand out under the pines. I could hear a strange sound. It was a lonesome sound, circling around the house four times. When she died I never heard that again.

Account 9

[Did someone witch your brother?]
Since he was three my brother got crippled. He used to *make money* dancin' and some didn't like it. He was a real good dancer. They think they know who done it to him [witched him] but they can't do nuthin' about it.

Account 10

[Informant brings out a yard of cord from inside a pillow in her house.] I got this one time years and years ago when I was witched through jealousy. A man came in my house one time and looked around and saw everythin' all nice and was jealous. After that I used to see a bird watchin' me; it was him. Then my throat and heart begun to hurt and my husband took me all over to doctors but they couldn't help me. Then that Chippewa—the one I told you about—called me up there. He took me in that tent [he was a Cese·ko] and gave me this to put on. Then he made the tent shake and I heard all sorts of shrieking voices and my throat got better. He said it was that bird's beak goin' back and forth from my throat to my heart. He told me to wear this whenever I travel and no harm can come to me when I have that on. I can tell whenever a witch is near when I'm wearin' it.

Account 11

They can't find the body [of the boy who drowned]. His dad used to *show off*. He wouldn't say "hello." But he talks different [now]. You should be good to people. . . .

The fear of an involvement with witchcraft among members of the native-oriented group is still very real. Very few witchcraft incidents were told by the men in this group, who are more directly involved with power gaining and power retention. A powerful male elder, who cautiously avoided speaking of witchcraft, remarked, "There are many things that I can't talk about; if we were to do so, it would take much time, a lot of tobacco, and a lot of money." Fear is probably greater today than previously since none of the younger men have undergone the Great Fast to receive a tutelary spirit (which protects one from evil powers, as well as bestowing special good powers upon one). Further, there are no powerful shamans left to combat the witch.

One is not personally responsible for the amount or kind of power that is bestowed upon him according to Menomini belief. The witch, therefore, cannot help that his tutelary spirit was evil or that he inherited evil powers. Many "good" old men and women have witch bags, but no one expressed a desire for receiving one. In fact, most informants expressed great fear of the bags and desired to burn or destroy them. One informant said, "I told S. not to take the bag [witch bag] if she wanted her family to grow up. Father said it wasn't right for people to have it. So she burned it. His bag harmed people. It was hidden." Another informant said, "My mother had one, but she didn't want it and put it in the swamp."

The attitude of the members of this group toward the witchcraft act itself is one of "passive acceptance," which also characterizes their attitude toward all supernatural powers. To a large extent, fate decrees whether or not a person will receive great powers. If he does not, there is little that he can do about it. Therefore, one accepts his lot. This "acceptant" attitude is illustrated in the remarks of a woman when she was asked why she had married a man whom she neither knew nor liked. She replied, in a matter-of-fact manner, that his (her husband's) old father would witch her if she did not.

Viewed in broad perspective, witchcraft might be thought of as a behavior pattern that contributes to the functioning of the group. It serves an "adaptive" function for the native-oriented group in that it insures social cooperation and preserves the status quo of the group by vesting the elders with special powers. In the absence of direct social controls exercised through positions of secular power, witchcraft and the threat of witchcraft serve as means of controlling or preventing behavior that is potentially disruptive in interpersonal relations. The structure of motivations and controls represented in the socially required values and psychological organization characteristic of individuals (equanimity under duress, latescence, control of emotionality and aggression, and autonomy) is congruent with this type of social control. Beliefs and participation in witchcraft, like beliefs and participation in religious patterns, both express basic processes in the native-oriented cultural system and serve to validate and maintain them.

Becoming a Menomini

ATTITUDES TOWARD CHILDREN

How are individuals with the values and psychological organization needed for the maintenance of the cultural system produced? In the native-oriented group of Menomini the influence of the culture on the child is apparent even before the child is born. The parents are expecting a reincarnated elder in the form of a baby and are prepared to treat the child as such. As one woman said, "I feel that sometimes a baby being born, maybe one of our grandfathers might have his spirit in the little boy." This means that the baby, like all elders, is a favored person to be shown special privileges. Children, like old people, are close to the supernatural, to the power that pervades all things and from which man receives life and energy. The autonomous attitude characteristic of native-oriented Menomini is expressed in the respect adults have for the possessions and rights of all children (see the quote on p. 22). As pointed out in an earlier section, children even receive equal shares of the earnings of the dance group, and the money is theirs to spend as they wish. Respect is also shown in the special observances for children. During the first year of life each child must be given

The young boys learn from the older men.

a name. An elder is requested to give the name, and it is bestowed at a feast given by the parents for as many people as they have food and place for. The elder gives the matter serious thought, sometimes mulling it over for several months. When he is ready, the feast is held. After the food is consumed he rises with the child in his arms and gives a talk, giving the name and explaining why it is selected and asking the spirits for a long life for the child. Sometimes the name is given in recognition of some special characteristic the elder believes he sees in the child. Other times the name of a deceased person is given in recognition of the possibility that his spirit has been born again in this child. This event is of great importance because if a child is not pleased with his name, he may depart to the spirit world from whence he came.

Children are carefully watched to see if they are at ease with their name. If one stands quietly in the midst of play, as though preoccupied with some inner distress, the parents will take the child to an elder, who will attempt to talk with it to see whether it has the right name. One family in the native-oriented group had a year-old daughter whose head shook. After several months a cousin said that she needed a different name. A feast was given and a powerful elder called in to rename her. The mother said, "That was all that was the matter. After she got her new name, her head stopped shaking."

If the child weeps ceaselessly, or is listless or sickly, obviously something is wrong and the worried parents send to the local doctor. Although the physician may try all his cures, they are in vain, the trouble is more deep seated, the doctor diagnoses the case as beyond his power and it is given to some old seer, preferably one of those gifted with the power to understand the languages of babies, which, while Menomini, is a peculiar dialect unintelligible except to the initiated. [Skinner 1913:37]

Respect and concern for children extends through all the years of growing up. When a boy kills his first game—no matter how small or large it is—a feast is held to celebrate this event and his praises are sung by all present. In the earlier days a formal rite was given at this time; most men in the native-oriented group remember this event as a less formal but still important occasion. One man related:

That old grandfather of mine tell me how to do . . . circle . . . if you see no tracks you know he isn't there. Circle around again. The deer knows you circle, he stay still. Sure enough, the second time I circle, I see the deer hiding, laying against a windfall, ears down. So I shot him in the head. First deer I ever killed. Gee! I was happy! First deer I killed. I start whooping, run home. My mother and grandmother was surprised. "Is it really so?" they kept asking. We took pack straps, knives, a little hatchet. I took them up there, sure enough, there he was. The old lady [grandmother] was pretty good. She cut it up and we packed it home. That was pretty good.

The women sliced it up good. They made sticks to roast the meat close to the fire. Then they cook what they eat. The ribs and chest they boil, the best part for them. Then the men folks come. We waiting for them. When they come in, the grandfather come first. He had nothing, just his gun and pack strap. He say, "Who that is?" The old lady, she laugh, "I guess your grandson beat you!" The grandfather say then, "Just for that we offer a prayer for to give thanks so this boy be a good hunter." So they all come; they was happy, for quite a while. We had a feast. We offer prayer . . . eat afterwards. I was fourteen when that happened. That I remember good.

This same attitude toward children extends to everyday matters. The little girl who fills her pail with wild blackberries is praised—but never in such a manner as to imply that she did better than someone else. When the boys and girls hop around the dance area in imitation of the adults, all the Menomini present whoop and clap as though the children had done something quite marvelous. Unlike the situation often existing in middle-class America, Menomini adults treat children supportively without "possessing" them.

CONSTRAINTS UPON BEHAVIOR AND SEX

How are the constraints so necessary to the maintenance of Menomini culture imposed upon the child? The child's first direct experience with restraint is with the swaddling cloths and blankets in which it is wrapped. The cradle board is no longer used, but children are enfolded in several layers of cloth, and are usually placed in a blanket that is folded in such a way that it can be tied at both ends and suspended as a hammock. Even on hot days babies are enclosed in this manner, sometimes with only the head and face peeking out of the tightly folded blanket. When a male baby is born, his penis is pinched by an old woman in attendance, usually one of his grandmothers, so that it will not grow to abnormal size and so that he will be able to control his passions when he grows to maturity. Doubtless this act has little direct effect on the child, but it is symbolic of the value placed upon control.

In other aspects of child care than those just described, however, children in the native-oriented group are treated with tolerance and permissiveness. They are nursed whenever they are hungry or whenever they fret. Weaning is gradual, and even children in the walking stage may be given the breast if they are ill or uneasy, and if there is milk. Toilet training is carried out casually. Children are encouraged to "hold back" when they can understand the reasons for doing so, but no particular fuss is made if they do not succeed. Menomini mothers are puzzled by the concern displayed by Whites over such matters.

Until the child can run about by itself, the mother, a grandmother, or an older sibling is always nearby. Infants and young children are held a great deal. Fathers and older brothers as well as mothers walk about holding children in their arms, even when talking with strangers. Apparently, it is assumed that everyone likes to hold babies because during a conversation the holder of a baby will hand it over to the person with whom he or she is talking without asking if the recipient of the frequently rather damp bundle wants to hold it. Despite the supportive holding of babies by almost everyone there is little demonstrative fondling, hugging, or kissing. Babies are frequently held facing away from the holder. In general the interaction rate between adults and young children seems low to the White observer. The behavior of the mother is aimed primarily at avoiding catastrophe such as the death of a child by neglecting to observe particular taboos, invoking the wrath of an unappeased elder reincarnated in a newborn baby, or experiencing power loss by not treating the child as he wishes to be treated. She must continually watch the baby for evidence of strange behaviors of any kind—undue sadness, excessive crying which may indicate that a reincarnated elder wishes a special naming ceremony and a change of name. When unusual signs appear, a feast must be given and a new name tried. Sometimes, this occurs several times.

Discipline is very mild. No adult in the native-oriented group remembers being whipped as a child, and none of them whip their children now. "They used to be good to me, never scold me, and I used to be good that way too. I never went through anything like being hit on the face . . . like I saw one White man do to his kid. He hit him right on the mouth, like he was a man," as one fifty-year-old man in the native-oriented group said.

Children are never struck until they are eight years of age. . . . Pulling a child's ears makes it scrofulous and striking it about the head makes it deaf and foolish. "Only White men are capable of such barbarities." [Skinner 1913:41]

Another man in his thirties relates, "I don't remember ever getting a real switching. Oh maybe just a little bit on the legs, that's all. When I didn't mind, like maybe I cried for some little thing, or they can't make me be still, or maybe I didn't listen to my ma, then maybe I got a dipper full [of cold water] in the face. Then I had to listen!"

> *Small children are scolded or a little water is thrown in their faces to wash away their trouble.* [Skinner 1913:41]

The attitude of adults toward children and the conception of proper treatment seem clear in the following comment by one middle-aged man:

> I remember how nice and quiet my uncle used to talk to me, so I always listen to what he say, and try to do what he want. So one time we took a boy [adopted one]. He was mean, used to run around, his parents treated him bad, but we treat him like my uncle treated me. We keep him clean . . . get food what's good for him. If he like something to eat, we get that for him. We try to keep him around us all the time. We think he get better if we treat him like that. After a while he did. He minded good, listened, try to do like we say.

> *Children under the protection of the gods must not be scolded until they are well grown, for they may become offended and go back to their friends or relations.* [Skinner 1913:40]

When a child is out of line and does not evidence sufficient control over his or her behavior, a most effective method for bringing him or her under control is to threaten him with the owl. The fear of the world of spirits and ghosts surrounding him is inculcated in the child at a very early age.

Children receive little instruction about sex—but they need little since its natural manifestations are apparent in the close quarters of a shack or hut. Masturbation is rather casually discouraged. Adults never expose their bodies in toto, but a woman will nurse a child in public with no concern. In the past the typical restrained attitude toward sex was manifested in the use of a *meˀnapos* blanket, a soft deerskin with a single hole in the middle, which covered the woman during intercourse and minimized direct contact. These blankets were used until very recent times by married couples, and the attitudes symbolized by their use are still a part of the value system of the native-oriented group.

> *. . . there was formerly a taboo against the contact of the skin of males and females. To obviate this difficulty Ma'nabus prepared a large buckskin, with a single perforation, to cover the woman. This robe was handed down to mankind and to comparatively recent times the custom was still in vogue among the Menomini.*
>
> *Certain persons in every band were granted, through their dreams, the right to possess these robes. The skins were beautifully painted and ornamented*

and kept as sacred articles, to be rented out to those who wished to use them. Anyone who wished to hire a blanket first approached the owner with a present of tobacco as a preface to his request and on its return another present had to be made in payment. If the users soiled the robe, an indemnity was demanded by the owner. [Skinner 1913:30–31]

SOCIAL PARTICIPATION

One of the most rewarding aspects of growing up in Menomini culture is the fact that a child is a participant in the important happenings of the group. When a Dream Dance is being held, all of the children down to the smallest baby are in the room where the service is conducted. Adults are tolerant of potential disruptions that would disturb Whites in similar circumstances. A baby that starts to fret when a prayer is being offered or a tobacco sacrifice is being made is held gently, given the breast, or carried out of the room without any visible tension or anger on the part of the mother or other attendant who carries it out. Very young children are encouraged to take part in the affair. Toddlers dance, held at first by their upraised arms by older brothers or sisters.

One eleven-year-old boy was given a regular place around the drum. He used his drumstick to help the fast-moving and highly synchronized beat, and tried to join in the rather complex and very quick-tempo songs. His beat was a little ragged, and his singing was far from being a positive contribution to the chorus, but the men carrying out the service treated him like a full member of the ritual group. His careful and self-conscious attempt to replicate every move and posture of the men, even the facial expressions, was an impressive demonstration of how learning occurs in this group. His youngest brother, age three and one half, ran over to him one night shortly after he took his place at the drum. The eleven-year-old promptly found a stool for him and gently sat the child on it next to him. The little boy sat on the stool quietly, absorbed by the activity, while two choruses were sung. Then he became restive and started to run about the room. His older brother got up, took him by the arm, and rather firmly sat him down again upon the stool. The little boy, unaccustomed to such firm treatment by his brother, started to sob quietly—apparently fighting for control but not quite achieving it. Finally, his brother took him by the hand, and with a very solicitous look upon his face, led him out of the room. The next time a song service was held, the little boy sat again upon the stool by the side of his older brother, but this time he stayed there quietly for about an hour, then got up and walked carefully over to his mother's side and climbed upon the bench beside her. At later services he took the same position by his brother during the early part of the evening. He had learned something. Seven years later he sat with his brother, now a young man, at the same drum, but now he had his own drumstick, and tried to sing, like his brother had before at the age of eleven.

This is the way roles are learned in the native-oriented group and one reason why the way of life of this group has persisted for so long in the face of intensive pressures for change from the outside world. In a small homogeneous

Younger children learn from older siblings.

group of this sort, the child is able to assume and understand the roles of every member of the group and to learn what the expectations of each member of the group are for him or her. As Margaret Mead once wrote, growing up in a homogeneous group allows for "effective *prefiguring of future experience* and reinforcement and consolidation of past experience" (Mead 1949:550).

STORYTELLING AND PREACHING

Native-oriented Menomini believe strongly in the power of the spoken word. As soon as children can understand, adults are constantly "putting a bug in your ear," as one young man expressed it. There are several different ways of putting a bug in. In the old days there was a regular cycle of stories and myths told through certain times of the year. Usually, some elder who was both powerful and wise would establish a special reputation as a good storyteller. He would hold forth by his hearth on certain evenings, and parents would bring their children to hear him. Older people in the present group remember these storytelling times when as many as twenty children might be listening at the same moment.

The mass of popular folklore is comprised in the group known as "true stories." While these are, for the most part, not sacred, they range from simple narratives of daily life to supernatural experiences. The former are droll, exciting, or explanations of natural phenomena. . . . They are told in public at any time when apropos, but generally around the fire in the evening. The latter are often in the nature of confidences, and are imparted only in private....

Naturally inclined to the dramatic, the Menomini embellish every myth and fairy tale with a richness of gesture and vocal inflection that cannot be transcribed on paper. The sign language, now almost obsolete as such, is still used to render the tales more graphic. A number of signs otherwise lost may be resurrected by a careful study of gestures used in story telling.

Every character in the story has its peculiarity of speech by which it is known, a fact that is true of Indian mythology in general to a much larger extent than has been recognized. These idiosyncrasies are mimicked by the narrator. [Skinner and Satterlee 1915:235]

Still today some Menomini elders tell stories "with a richness of gesture and vocal inflection that cannot be transcribed on paper." The type of stories remembered by the older and middle-aged people today as most entertaining consist of stories about various wizards and heroes and their exploits; stories of war, hunting, love, ghosts, and magic; and stories about "how the skunk got his stripes" and "how the crane got the black ring around his neck." The other major type of story includes the cosmogonic myths—the origin of the Menomini; the nature of the stratified universe and the beings in it; and, particularly, the *Meʔnapos* cycle, stories about the culture hero of the Menomini who was part hero and part buffoon. This latter category of stories were told in a more serious vein, usually to older children and during a period of weeks when the cycle would not be interrupted.

The most basic Menomini values, such as the relationship of power to the entire system of belief and action, are represented in these stories. In the myths the hero is helpless without his dream-bestowed and ritually maintained power, and he may lose it by abuse, neglect, or lack of constraint. However, the hero is particularly successful only because he has acquired a certain power. In contests between great shamans, one of the contestants may realize and admit that his power is not strong enough to withstand that of the other so he gives in without further struggle. The individual is dependent upon this power as something beyond himself—something gained by him through proper behavior. This attitude, as described earlier, persists today among the members of the native-oriented group. Many of the tales contain explicit or implicit rules for behavior which are accepted today: A good man is brave, respects the rights of others, and does not arouse antagonisms; he lives quietly and observes the sacrifices required to maintain good relations with the powers; and he is modest, even tempered, and guards himself against undue pride.

Today the children do not have the opportunity to hear these same stories and myths told in their fullness and richness, but all children in the native-oriented group have heard stories. The content is attenuated, but the themes are recognizable. For example, one night a man in his late thirties was telling his children about a great hunter. He always got his bag full of ducks. He went out to his favorite spot and waited for the ducks to fly in during the half-light moments of dawn. Suddenly, there was a rush of wings as a flight settled in before his hiding place. He rose to shoot, but slipped and fell, discharging his shotgun harmlessly in the air. The ducks all rose in a flurry of beating wings. One big black duck, however, stayed on the water. The great hunter reloaded his gun and shot the unfortunate laggard. To his consternation he saw that he had shot his own hat, which had flown off his head when he fell down, and it floated, crownless and tattered, on the surface of the water. The great hunter went home, disgusted. That evening, as though to remind him of his ineptness, a large crane flapped past his house by the river, wearing the brim of his hat around his neck. Now every time he sees the ring-necked crane, he is reminded of his clumsiness on that morning.

Grandparents still tell children "bedtime stories," and the adults in the group remember when their grandparents told them stories. "Grandmaw told us kids a story every night before we went to sleep. First thing next morning she would ask us what the story was about. If we couldn't tell her, she would tell the same story again the next night. She would do that until we could tell her what the story was about." What the grandmother was looking for was the moral point of the story, "that we shouldn't offend anybody's feelings," or "not to envy what someone else has got."

Adults seem to always be ready to point out a moral to children. One little boy stood by the window looking longingly out at the blizzardy landscape. "Gee, I wish it would get clear so I could go out and play tomorrow," he said. The next day dawned with a bright sun and he could go out. Before he did, however, his mother pointed out to him that he had asked for such weather the day before, and this showed that one should never wish for things unless one really wanted them to happen. Frequently, the moral point will be made with a proverb: "He who brags bites his own tail." "People who mind others' business get long noses." One who talks too much will get a big mouth." "He who spits at him gives him his life."

The constraint so necessary to the maintenance of the Menomini cultural system is sometimes taught directly. One young woman relates:

> He, my father, did right and treated all people the same. He was kind to everybody. Even the children today brag about my father. My father always made us sit every time we ate anything. He said the food wouldn't do no good otherwise. He said we would be just like horses, running around and eating, and our food wouldn't do us no good. We had to sit a while after we ate to let our food digest. We could never talk very much while we was at the table. He didn't even like us to stretch or things like that after we ate. I used to think my father was awful hard on us, but I can see now, that he was just tryin' to raise us right and teach us the right things to do. So I keep tellin' my children the same things as my father told us. [L. Spindler, field notes]

Children are taught to be quiet and not ask a lot of questions. "Sit quiet like a stone, and let thoughts come to you. Think about a leaf in a pool." Children are taught explicitly to be generous and respect old people: "Father said, 'Live

in peace. Be good to every person. If you live somewhere . . . if you have something to eat . . . feed him . . . even though there is only one meal in your house,
feed him anyway, especially if it's an old lady or an old man.' "

Much of the moral instruction given a child is formalized in the "preach-
ings" that every Menomini child is supposed to receive from an older person,
usually a grandparent, starting at about age eight. Grandparents have already
played a very important role in the child's education before that time. Children
spend almost as much time with their grandparents (particularly on the mother's
side) as they do with their parents, and sometimes considerably more. Menomini
mothers have always claimed a rather high degree of freedom. They dance, help
collect greens and ferns, hunt and fish, and travel; to increase freedom of movement, children will sometimes be left with grandparents. The attachment to the
older people on the part of the children is usually great, but it is given a special
character by the respect toward and fear of old people as retainers of great
supernatural power. Children are taught never to irritate old people, not to stare
at them, or talk loudly around them. They are told to fill their pipes, run errands
for them, and never hurt their feelings. In the words of some of the present-day
native-oriented Menomini quoted previously:

Another thing they [parents] used to say if you hurt old men's feelings,
your child might die and hurt your feelings.

My father used to tell us we were supposed to always help out old people
and do all we can and never make a fuss, because some day you might come
across some old person who might happen to have that bag [witch bag].

The child had to sit still [at meetings], because if it would stare at some
person, the person wouldn't like it. My mother never took us anyplace.

It is never forgotten that all old people are potential witches. So children
listen well to their grandparents. When the child reaches the eighth year, it is
believed that he is no longer likely to want to go back to the spirit world. His
own spirit is satisfied with the treatment it has received. So it is now time to
lay out the virtues he is expected to acquire and live by in a more directive
fashion than heretofore. This preaching continues, with content appropriate to
age and role, until the youngsters are married.

Grandmothers tell young girls that they will be getting married someday.
They should look after their husbands, keep their clothes well, put good food
on the table, not be lazy around the house. They should avoid love potions to
get or hold him because these potions are dangerous and may kill him, or cause
him to become so jealous that he will kill her.

Father used to preach to us to understand things. He was always yelling and
preachin'. But now today, I'm glad he done those thing. He never liked love
medicine. He said "Whenever you get married and can't seem to hold your
husband, don't start askin' for love powder. If you use it on him, he won't be

in his right mind. I'll tell you one good thing on how to hold your man. Keep his table full and keep his clothes good."

My mother did a lot of preachin'. . . . When I married B., she said, "Always be good to that old lady [mother-in-law]. Beat her up in the morning and get breakfast and do what she says. Don't lie around and look at books or anything like that. Get up early and work real hard, then she won't get mad at you. If she does, she won't hurt you, but she'll get someone you like best like your brother or mother or sister."

He [father] told me to always treat my in-laws good and to be good to my husband. That's why J. and me get along so good. We been married twelve years now.

Young girls were told that a menstruating woman is dangerous, that when she menstruates the first time, she will be given utensils of her own to cook with, and that she should stay away from men and children during her menstrual period thereafter to avoid causing them to become ill or die.

. . . I am always careful about eatin'. I cooked by myself and used my own pots and pans. . . . Some have two stoves. They're all careful at that time not to eat among others or the old folks will get sick . . . it would kill them [their guardian spirit], or give them diarrhea or something. When a girl gets that way, we was all told that for one year not to touch a baby. Some old person's spirit is in a little baby and she might kill them.

[Did your mother have you go off by yourself when you began to menstruate?]
Every month I was home [from school] I did my own cookin' off by myself, away from the house with my own dishes. It wasn't bad. It was kinda fun. . . . We had to be real careful about where we stepped at that time and about feedin' babies.

Young Menomini girls are told about the penalties of loose sexual behavior and that when they are married, their husband can tell "if they have been good."

Well, you know, she [aunt] started telling me about married life first. She said, "Some day some man will come," and said, "If you want to get married, you should behave and not run around and have things to do with other fellows. If you do get married and have done bad things, your husband will find out and pick on you and you'll never get along after that. If you behave and wait until you're really married, your husband will have nothing against you and you'll get along. Your husband can tell if you was good or not."

My grandmother used to scare me half to death about goin' around boys. She used to say, "Your tits will get real long and heavy and hang down if you go around boys before you're married." Then they used to say a boy's tits would get big too if he hung around girls.

A man got the same preachin' to. He was supposed to do the same as the girls. It wouldn't matter as much, though. They would tell him that some fellows have children and don't marry the girls and that he would be having children with no one to take care of them.

Girls were instructed about medicines that can cause abortion if used during the first few weeks of pregnancy and about medicines for taking after the birth of a child.

There is Indian medicine. A bitter root, like a physic. It's better to take it the first month. If two or three pass, the woman doesn't know if she will die.

Some medicines we drink for one month after we have our babies. You have to add fruit trees (roots) to the medicine, wash roots, pound. Take apple tree, wash that, tie up with string, let dry until it's easy to pound, tie each up separate. When dry, take one root, pound up, sift, put aside, then take next [raspberry], keep on, then mix all fine stuff together, then put away in jar. This will be for after a baby.

Young people are given rather elaborate directions for making medicines when they are initiated into the Medicine Lodge:

We don't allow any kind of bad medicine [in the Lodge]. After my mother died, I took out her medicine. When they put me in [initiated me], each put a medicine in that bag . . . one for headaches—sneezing medicine. Another gave me something for diarrhea. Eight old men and two women gave me medicine. They pound all medicines together and mix them together. I got to keep track so I write down what they're for. There was one old fellow from Wabeno who gave me medicine in case someone ever dopes you with love powder. You put it in the middle of your head and you'll be back to normal. They give you just a little, like samples, then you go to them to find out how it's made. You sample it first, if it's good, then go to the person to learn.

A transitional woman who was raised by a native-oriented grandmother, known as a doctor with powerful medicines, learned about medicines from her. She then began to practice medicine herself.

I know lots of good medicines. If you got some cancer on your skin, you take the skin of a frog and put over it and it takes it all up when you pull it off. If there is some left, you just pick it off with tweezers. If it's inside you, you find some rotten log and boil it up into tea and keep drinkin' that.

Those medicines my grandmother told me about all came to me later in a
dream and I did lots of doctorin' all around.

Young girls are told by the elders to always treat their husbands the
same way whether he is drunk or sober. One woman describes how she con-
tinuously took her husband back after his sprees in a patient, acceptant manner.

He [husband] used to drink and leave me when I had my babies—a boy
and then twins. He done a lot of drinkin' and ran around with women. He
lived with a Oneida woman for two weeks. . . . When we came here he started
that up again and left me and never came home. . . . I had to stay by myself
because I wasn't divorced. I wanted to see what J. [husband] was going to do.
[Why?]
I suppose I'd have to take him back if he wanted to.

Grandfathers also tell young boys to be generous, to feed old people.
They tell them not to boast of their exploits or abilities and never to envy someone else's abilities. Boys are cautioned about looking for bad medicines and are
told to keep away from menstruating women. They are told about their obligations to in-laws and their responsibilities to any guardian spirits they may have
inherited. They are warned about sex and the diseases that can come as a result
of dalliance. They are told to treat their wives well and cautioned about the
danger that sorcery may be directed at them by the wife's parents if they do
not. They are told to mind their own business and never to talk carelessly about
important things like religion or the spirits.

In former times this period of being "preached to" would have been cli-
maxed by the puberty fast, followed by an intensive period of instruction on
the esoteric and sacred aspects of Menomini belief. Individuals who received
unusual guardians or vision experiences would be given prolonged and specialized
instruction, with all of the details of ritual and cosmogonic rationale, by an old
man who was one or another kind of "medicine man." Today the puberty fast
is no longer possible for the young people, and even though there is continuity
in the way individuals maintain sacred power and the expectations people have
concerning it, the loss of the puberty fast is a serious blow to the efficacy of the
native-oriented educational system. Adolescent education is the weakest link in
the process today, and it is during adolescence that young people frequently move
away from the native-oriented group into the transitional and acculturation-oriented
groups in the Menomini community. The native-oriented group is shrinking but
shows surprising strength in view of the predictions made by every student of
Menomini culture since 1890 that the Menomini culture would disappear completely during the next decade or so. This ability to survive is related to the
effectiveness of the educational system just described.

Why do Menomini children grow up, within the native-oriented framework, exhibiting the socially required behaviors and psychological orientations
—autonomy, equanimity under duress, latescence, and emotional control? One
answer is that they grow up this way because there is no reason for them not

to. These qualities are taught—directly and indirectly in the way young children are induced into more advanced roles, in the things children hear elders saying at ceremonials, in the moral points underscored again and again by parents and grandparents with a definite point of view, making observations and reinforcing behavior in different contexts as events occur that lend themselves to such interpretation. They are taught in myths and stories told now in attenuated but recognizable form. They are revitalized and encapsulated in highly explicit preaching by respected and feared mentors during the period of most intense development just before and into early adolescence.

Menomini children early in their experience encounter all of the statuses and roles constituting, in their arrangement, the social structure of their society. This minimizes anxiety-arousing and frustrating discontinuities in education and experience. Discontinuities do exist, however, since children must attend schools run by White men and women with very different ideas about proper behavior than the children's parents have. In spite of these potentially conflict-laden situations, the educational experience for children in the native-oriented group has been successfully refractive in many cases to the impact of the educational experience contrived by agents of the dominant society. Adults who have undergone a tradition-oriented socialization experience in childhood, including the learning of the Menomini language, rarely (possibly never) are psychologically reoriented in maturity, even though they may take on specialized occupational roles and acquire the accessory behaviors necessary to get along in today's world.

Perhaps the most important factor in the success of the educational system is the fact that children in this society do not grow up resisting what they are being taught or the cultural agents doing the teaching. The encounters they have had with cultural agents (parents, grandparents, aunts, elders) during the early years of experience have been more than favorable—they are designed to make children feel "at home," to make them want to stay. Children are treated with tolerance and supportiveness. It is true that these are qualities in varying degrees characteristic of many nonliterate groups, but Menomini children are treated with special respect. Respect, even for children, is probably characteristic of social systems exhibiting a high degree of individual autonomy. In the Menomini case this feature is emphasized and reinforced by the belief that children and old people possess the greatest power and are closest to the supernatural. This respect, however, does not result in complete permissiveness. There is gentle, constant, consistent discipline in the restraints with which children are surrounded. At the same time Menomini children are supported and rarely threatened by authoritarian demands or crude violations of their person in the form of physical punishment. Most encounters with cultural agents during the early years of life are favorable and, as a result, the child is open and receptive to learning and to becoming what the carriers of his culture want him to be.

The discontinuity between experience in Whiteman schools and that in the Menomini family and home was very great. Euro-American concepts of child training and education are radically divergent from those of the traditional Menomini. Strict discipline, abrupt interference with the child's activities, use of crticism rather than praise, and corporal punishment were foreign to the Meno-

mini and were interpreted by them as lack of respect for the child, if not down-
right cruelty. Our case histories contain instances of shocked parents who tried
to protect their children, sometimes by removing them from school and from
what they saw as harsh and unnecessary behavior on the part of teachers and
school administrators. The culturally patterned tendencies of Whiteman school
personnel were reinforced by prejudice on the part of Whites toward Indians.
These conditions have surely ameliorated in recent years, and in any event by
now many, if not most, Menomini have become callous to violations of this sort
as they have become acculturated, so the discontinuity is not so great as it was
a generation ago. However, the initial discongruity between Whiteman and
Menomini concepts of a good education have played a determinant role in the
long-term, fundamental educational failure of the Whiteman schools, for Menomini
as well as other Indians (See B. Berry, 1969).

Conclusion

In this chapter we have described and interpreted the first of the adaptive
strategies represented by the various acculturative groups of Menomini. In doing
so we have moved back and forth between past and present to give depth and
completeness to the cultural and psychological features that tie the Menomini
to their own origins. However, this technique of presentation should not be allowed to obscure the fact that the native-oriented group is an adaptation to the
prolonged confrontation of the Menomini and Whiteman cultural systems. We
have tried to make this clear as we have proceeded, but we reemphasize it now,
for it is a crucial point in our analysis. The native-oriented cultural system is an
attempt to maintain a way of life that is dying. The majority of the men in it
under fifty had a Whiteman school experience superimposed upon the traditional education we have described, and fairly extensive experience in the outside
world. They chose to identify with the native-oriented group, and to become
members of the ceremonial organizations. This is less true of the women, for
they have had, as a rule, less outside experience, but their self-consciousness about
their identity is clear. The native-oriented group is literally a reaffirmative movement on a small scale. Its religions, dances and songs, witchcraft, and myths and
stories are all affirmations of a cultural system that is highly discongruent with
that of the Whiteman. The people in it, with the exception of the elders, who
have known little else and are heuristically native oriented, are maintaining
control and identity by reasserting one way of life and attempting to exclude the
other, in its most disruptive moral and philosophical forms. They are, of course,
only partially successful. In the long run the attempt seems doomed, but the
attempt is interesting and significant, for it is one of the ways in which people
in such a situation attempt to cope with the exigencies of cultural confrontation
between discongruent cultural systems, either between separate, or formerly separate, societies, or within one large society.

In the next chapter we will consider an alternative adaptive strategy in
which Menomini have engaged—the Peyote church. Though basically native-

oriented in its premises about the nature of man, life, spirit, and power, Peyotism is a move toward a synthesis with limited aspects of Whiteman culture.[17]

---

[17] Rorschachs and interviews were conducted with, and observations made of, nearly all active adult members of both the native-oriented group and the separate group of Peyotists. The same is true of the elite acculturated group. The transitionals and the lower-status acculturated groups are sampled less adequately, due to the sheer size of the population in these categories. Details can be found in G. Spindler and L. Spindler 1970.

3

The Peyote Road

The Ideology

PEYOTISM is an intensely personal experience. This is so even though there is a high degree of patterning in ritual, symbolism, and belief that is both specific to the Menomini and shared widely with other Indians in North America. Each convert to Peyotism is searching for something. We see Peyotism as an adaptive strategy, as a way of reducing cognitive and emotional conflicts stemming from the confrontation between Menomini and Whiteman cultures. This is a conceptualization, an abstraction from specific events and individuals. To the individual the Peyote Road is a means to salvation, a resolution of personal conflict, a way of life, and a religion.

It is appropriate that the Peyotists should speak for themselves. Though we will interpret what they say in terms of our framework, much of this chapter has been "written" by the Peyotists themselves, as their statements were recorded by the Spindlers and by J. S. Slotkin.[1] This way the motivations and perceptions of the people may be understood. Our first concern is with the ideology of Menomini Peyotism.

1. We speak to Almighty God in our native tongue. God has given me His name in my language, *Kesɛ·maneto·w*, it means God, you know. He has given it to me. And I can pray to Almighty God right here in my own tongue because He has given it to me that way. And he teaches me that, in Peyote meetings. He doesn't teach me that in other religions, you know. For instance, this Catholic church, it doesn't teach me that way. There those prayers are already printed by some smart man; all you got to do is repeat it, and learn

---

[1] J. S. Slotkin, aided by his wife, Elizabeth Slotkin, worked with the Peyotists in 1951, and subsequently became a member of the Native American Church and a delegate to the national meetings of the organization. His most important publications are *Menomini Peyotism* (1952) and *The Peyote Religion* (1956). We worked independently and our results complement rather than contradict each other.

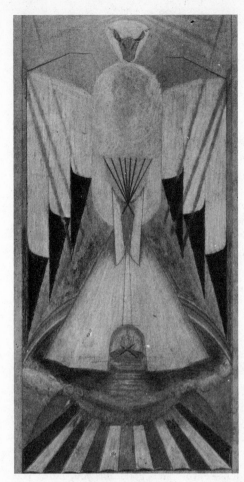

A crayon drawing by a Menomini
Peyotist, Mr. Star Shoshey. The
tepee is shown supported by the sun
and its rays, leading as paths to the
door, and protected by the Waterbird, with the head of the lamb of
peace.

it, and memorize it. That ain't no prayer for me. If I'm going to talk to God,
I must talk to Him right away from my heart; I must tell Him just what I
think, and what's troubling me. And I think the Peyote does that for me.
[Peyotist, in Slotkin 1952:617]

2. I'm going to tell you. Indians [are] awful poor; you know that yourself.
It's pretty hard, it's pretty hard to understand. Some of the Indians, some of
them, they don't believe God; they don't believe what these white people
believe. But this stuff here [peyote], if you use it, you'll think, "I wish we
get benefit from God." We pray. We know we're poor. But at the same time,
I wish we save our souls when we die. That's all we want. The rest, we don't
care; we can't get it. Even if the government, if we ask something—we have
a council—we don't get it. . . . [Peyotist, in Slotkin 1952:607]

3. I went to a meeting to find out about Peyote. After I had taken a few
herbs I saw a book open before me, with several verses in it. There was
something above that, too, but I couldn't seem to look up. It said in the book:
"Follow the path of Peyote, it is the only true path to me." Then a hand

came into my sight, and this hand pointed to the herb and a voice said, "Take of this, it is the true way." [Peyotist, in G. Spindler, field notes][2]

4.   What I tell you ain't gonna be much. I know only just some. I've been in this a long time, but I still know just some, not much. Some of the old people been learning this for fifty to sixty years know more, but still, they not know it all. When they learn about it they ready to go. They're all finished here. Why you want this? You gonna do anything? This other fellow [J. S. Slotkin] wants to find out about Peyote too. I told him, "You come to meetings, you learn there! I can't tell much like this. If you and I sit there all night, eat peyote, we can talk the next morning. You learn for yourself what it means." [Peyotist, in G. Spindler, field notes]

5.   There ain't no preaching in our ceremony. We get our knowledge from the Almighty direct. We don't need nobody telling us what the word is. That's what peyote is for. You take that, and the medicine will do the rest. God will talk to you himself. You don't need no bible. [Peyotist, in G. Spindler, field notes]

6.   I used to run around, drink, act wrong lots of times. I didn't take this religion seriously. But then I changed. I used to go to the meetings, sit there, take one or two peyote, not really work into it like I should. Then I started thinking. I gave up all this drinking. I went to meetings, prayed right, thought, took lots of peyote. I got a boy in Waukeshaw [state prison]. If he had followed me he would have been alright, but he wouldn't listen. [Peyotist, in G. Spindler, field notes]

7.   This here is the Indian religion—Peyote. It's good for you, cures you when you ain't well and it gives you knowledge. Things you never knew before you know when you eat that herb. The only way to know about peyote is to take it, it is the only way to learn. You eat the herb and sit there all night and sing and you learn things that you never knew before. There's an old man here who has taken it for a long time. He learned all that is in the Bible by taking the herb. He can't read or write and he never seen a Bible but he can tell you everything that's in it because of peyote. He even knows some things that's supposed to be in the Bible that ain't; things you White men forgot when you wrote the Bible; things you left out when you went from the Old Testament to the New Testament. He can tell what's going to happen too. It's our religion, we don't need no White man stuff. Them nuns ought to go away, we don't need them. We don't want White men around when we take peyote; we let Spindler in and he took some too, but I don't think he learned nothing. [From a Peyotist's responses to the values picture study technique administered by Robert Edgerton to respondents from the Spindler acculturation sample (Goldschmidt and Edgerton 1961)]

---

[2] The full texts for these and other Peyotists who gave accounts of their beliefs and experiences to the Spindlers are available in the *Microcard Publications of Primary Records in Culture and Personality*, B. Kaplan, ed., 1958.

8. Almost reminds me of our fire place . . . that you seen last Sunday. The fire is right in here . . . or the ashes of it. You know . . . this fire here . . . it goes right up like that. If you do something wrong in everyday life it goes right through there. [Question] Here's the fireplace, and the trail that goes in there. We get rid of our sin in that fire, and the trail goes right through. [Question] These could be angels, watching the fire from each side. That's the way they're shaped. [Peyotist response to card I of the Rorschach, in G. Spindler, field notes]

9. Jesus Christ, tell me what our all-in-all father, Great Spirit, wants of me. And as for this medicine here, that was found here where we live, these [rites] are according to the commandments of Great Spirit, our father, so that we should know what must be done. It is the commandment of our all-in-all father, Great Spirit.

And again, he really sent you here, Jesus Christ, when you walked around here where we live, in order to teach us the way we should live. Now then, I thank you for teaching us about this medicine.

Well then, pray to this medicine, so that we will know how to act as we should according to the commandments of our all-in-all father, Great Spirit. This [Peyote] led the way for us which we should follow; it is a good way, one on which there is light. You [Peyote] are helping us so that we can learn that which we should follow. That is what I am praying for, Peyote. And that you will teach us how to behave when something is tempting us. Also that when we are ill it [Peyote] will heal us properly, so we will stand up straight and awaken well. That is what I ask of you; that you will help us.

I thank Great Spirit, our father, for his commandments from which we have learned. [An excerpt from a much longer prayer by the leader of a Peyote ceremony blessing the peyote to be distributed and asking that the purpose of the meeting be fulfilled. It was given in Menomini, translated by Slotkin (1952:593). Slotkin notes that during this prayer the leader "breaks down and weeps three different times."]

10. You [white people] want everything! He give us here, this earth; now white man take away from us—just where we got this little place here, what we live on now, to take away from us. [From a Peyotist's conversation with J. S. Slotkin (1952:608)]

11. It seems like—speaking about this Native American Church—the white man—what he did years ago, years back, way back in the beginning —he was supposed to come here, in the first place, to help these Indians. But instead of that he kind of turned around and beat him [out of] his country; seemed like he take everything away from him. Now, today, we see this Menomini reservation—still some Menomini here—well in the first place, this is their country! Not only this reservation, but they own the whole of North America. Now today [they own] just this little piece of land here. And through this Native American Church, it seems like the foundation is coming out somewhere. Seem like you going to find that foundation, what belongs to the

Indian. In other words, it seems like you're going to come here, and you're going to take that away from them, and take it away to the old country. Kind of looks that way, too. [Peyotist, in Slotkin 1952:622]

12. That night the medicine worked on me. Pretty soon I see what looks like a mountain shaped like that moon [the half-moon altar] . . . it looked like a great big mountain. Pretty soon it seemed like I was on top of it. Then I turned around and I could see something going, like the way it's supposed to in meetings. Pretty soon I see somebody, he had on dark pants and a white T-shirt and some kind of cap, like a police cap. He looks like he was standing on top of the world, in the East I could see that . . . the world and him standing on top of it. He must be real powerful, I thought, whoever he is. Then he was moving his arms, back and forth, stretching. Then, all of a sudden, I could feel him hitting me. "I got to pound that good stuff into you!" It was that Peyote. It was him. [Peyotist, in G. Spindler, field notes]

13. . . . because I'm weak; and if I'm weak, well, I got to use that [peyote], because there's mɛ·skowesan [power] in there, in that medicine. [Question] From the Almighty; they got it from there, mɛ·skowesan; he put it down there in that Peyote. [Excerpted from a longer conversation about various forms of power and their relationship with peyote between a Peyotist and J. S. Slotkin (1952:641)]

14. My old aunt was the one. My mother died when I was little and this aunt raised me. I lived with her. That was when I had my other wife, that's dead now. . . . I used to go to all this powwow doings. I never knew what it was all about. I never prayed or nothing. I just go to have a good time . . . never heard a word about God . . . same with metɛ·wen too. I just sang songs, danced, listened to the drum. I never thought about what any of it meant. Then one day (I was about twenty-nine at time) my old aunt called me over to a meeting. She handed me a big dipper full of tea. She said to me, "Drink that, it's something good. I want you to have this." Well, I couldn't hardly say no to her. So, "Alright," and I took it down. Then later I had some more, another big dipper full of tea. I sat there all night, and listened to them praying. Everything was good, *good*, just right. . . . So that's how I got started. I learned about God. I thought a lot about it. I prayed. After I got into that I pulled away from the powwow and metɛ·wen, and all that stuff. [Peyotist, in G. Spindler, field notes]

15. We had a meeting up to Hayward, so I went up there. They had a tepee and everything, just like we do. I went in there, prayed, sang, like you seen. Then after midnight, that's a good time, suddenly I hear something . . . a sound . . . kind of a ring, like if when those telephone wires get hit by something. It got louder and louder. I was just sitting there, then a light from far off, way up, like a star . . . like as if I was outdoors like now, came towards me. It come fast, coming right towards me. Then it come real close, right up in front of me, and busted . . . just like one of them fireworks. It come up to

me and busted, all in little pieces of light. [Colored?] No, not colored, just bright light. I could see everything clear. That was good. That meant everything was going alright. It was a message from heaven. It showed me that I was doing good, doing the right thing, that I should keep on.

One other time I remember that was best. This was about ten years ago . . . in a meeting like the other one. I eat peyote all evening until midnight. I thought about my life, what I done . . . everything. Then midnight I went out for a little while . . . it's alright then . . . a intermission. I stand out there by myself, all alone. Then I heard that sound again, like I told you before . . . way up . . . loud and high. Then suddenly I hear another sound, like birds make when they fly . . . "swish, swish" . . . and somehow I could feel their wings on my face. I wondered what that was. I stood there and thought about it. Then, again, suddenly, I hear the same sound as before . . . that was something. I wondered. Then it came to me what it was; it was angels, come down from heaven. They come to show me our prayers was good, that God was listening. [Peyotist, in G. Spindler, field notes]

Certain themes appear in the statements above which occur in some form in most conversations with Menomini Peyotists. These recurrent themes do not appear to be specific to the Menomini, for Winnebago Peyotists whom we interviewed expressed them, and they are contained, in varying degrees of explicitness, in accounts from other tribes. This is not surprising, for Peyotism is today the most widely shared "Indian" religion in North America. It apparently diffused from the Kiowa-Comanche during the late nineteenth century. They in turn received it from the Apache, who got it from Mexico.[3] The Menomini received it in 1914 from a Potowatomi Peyote missionary, who lived for a time with a Menomini family who had become disaffected with the Dream Dance and Medicine Lodge and had moved away from the rest of the conservative group around Zoar. Use of peyote as a sacrament in a religious ceremony is pre-Columbian, but the present ideology and ceremony are a product of recent history, built upon a traditional cultural foundation. The present ritual in both the cross-fireplace and half-moon altar forms is composed of a medley of elements, many of apparent Plains Indian origin and some of Christian origin. The ritual and the supporting ideology are clearly a response to the defeat, deprivation, and confinement which Indians experienced nearly everywhere after the first half of the nineteenth century. We paraphrase and summarize this ideology as follows:

Peyote is God's (Great, or All-in-All Spirit *Kese·maneto·w*) gift to the Indian. The Whiteman has everything else. He has the Indian's land, his forests, and now he even wants to take away the land he gave the Indian by treaty. He is rich, he has fine clothes, money, cars, big houses, much furniture, much education. But the Indian has peyote, to give him the power of the Holy Spirit and cure him of sickness. (See statements 2, 7, 10, and 11.)

Peyote is a means to salvation after the ignorance of the days of the Medi-

---

[3] There are arguments about the exact origin of Peyotism which are well summarized by Weston LaBarre (1960).

cine Dance or after the sinfulness of one's previous life. It pulls men up from the dark pit. It shows them the light, the path to salvation and right living. (See statements 3, 6, 8, 9, and 14.)

By taking peyote at the meetings one can acquire some of the power put in the sacrament by the Great Spirit. (See statements 7, 12, and 13.)

Peyote gives one knowledge—of oneself as well as of heaven and earth and other things beyond ordinary knowledge. Peyote makes one think about oneself, all that one has done, all one's past life. (See statements 6, 7, and 15.)

One can learn only by taking peyote. It does no good to talk about it, or try to find out about it by reading books. Peyote is the teacher. (See statements 1, 3, 4, 5, 7, and 9.)

After years of going to meetings and partaking of peyote you will know only a little bit. No one knows very much. All the people are ignorant, but the ones who go to many meetings, pray, and take much peyote, and think about their past lives, are the only ones who know anything. (See statement 4.)

This ideology says much about the appeal and the functions of Peyotism as a response to the confrontation of Menomini and Whiteman culture. It appears to be a response to deprivation ("the Whiteman has everything else"), and it offers the security of knowledge and power and is a possession of the Indian. It offers salvation—the resolution of self-doubt and conflict about right and wrong, reflecting the discongruent demands issuing from native versus Whiteman culture, and reassurance that one is "doing right." We will observe the ramifications of this ideology in its functional context in the further explanations by Peyotists, and the observations of the ethnographers, to follow. The next section will deal with the Peyote ritual, its setting, paraphernalia, and ascribed meanings.

The Peyote Ritual and Meeting

Ceremonies are held in a large white tepee of the Plains type made of muslin sheeting or canvas in the yard of the person giving the meeting during warm weather, but during winter they are held in homes. The tepee is always oriented with the "door," frequently with a "caboose" (wall tent) entrance, to the east. The leader of the ceremony always sits directly across from the entrance. The tepee meeting begins with an opening prayer outside the tepee at sundown on Saturday and ends in the early hours of Sunday morning. It is usually called by one of the members for a declared purpose. The family giving the meeting furnishes a prepared tepee ground, and with the help of the officers appointed for the ceremony, puts up the tepee and arranges cedar boughs around the circular seating space inside and splits 4-foot lengths of ash firewood. The sponsoring family also provides most or all of the food consumed the next day by the participants who stay on.

After the opening prayer the leader (*meya·we·w*) or "chairman" requested by the sponsors enters first, then the rest of the assemblage enter. The men sit in the circle of the tepee on the cedar boughs and blankets. Their wives, if present, sit in back of them, half-crouched against the sloping tepee poles. The meeting

The tepee.

is then opened by the leader, who asks the person giving it to explain its purpose. When he is finished, the leader announces appointments to the places of drum chief, cedar man, fire tender, and sometimes waiter, gives the first prayer, and explains the procedure for the night. Then the peyote is passed, first (sometimes) in ground and moistened form, then in solid buttons. Each person may take as many as he wishes the second time, but usually only four the first. (The peyote is passed four times throughout the whole service.) With this, the singing and drumming begin, each man taking the staff and gourd rattle as he sings. He is accompanied by the rapid beat of the Peyote drum—a small copper kettle with a head of tautly drawn tanned buckskin and with an inch or two of water in the bottom—played either by a regular partner or by the man seated next to him. The drum, staff, and rattle are passed from man to man, clockwise, as each sings four songs. There is a recess (*nawa·c ape·w*, "he is there for awhile")[4] around midnight, and another pause about 3:00 A.M., which is marked by the prayer of the cedar chief. The ceremony ends at sunrise with consumption of blessed water and a communion breakfast (*mi·p me·cehsiya*, "we eat early in the morning"). Most participants and their families stay on the next day for a later, more substantial breakfast and dinner.

---

[4] For the accurate phonetic spelling and translation of this and many other Menomini terms we are indebted to J. S. Slotkin (1952).

In the center of the tepee ground is a carefully laid fire of clean split staves, the ashes of which are swept at dawn into the form of a dove or Waterbird. There is a half-moon altar of sand between the leader's place and the hearth, with a small pedestal for the "chief" peyote, and an indented line drawn along the top of the half-moon's ridge to symbolize the difficult and narrow path the Peyote member must follow through life. Material paraphernalia used during the meeting include the drum, a staff held by each singer in turn, and a gourd rattle to accompany his singing (together with the drum used by his "partner"), an eagle-feather fan, a bunch of sage, a small cloth bag for the cedar (dried, crumbled sprigs used as "incense"), a whistle made from the wing bone of an eagle, a larger cloth bag for the peyote that will be consumed during the evening, and the "master" or chief peyote (*oke·ma·w maski·hkiw*), an unusually large and perfectly formed peyote button kept in a buckskin bag. The leader usually has his own "kit" of "tools," kept in a small suitcase or (in one instance) a musical instrument case, and placed before him in careful order upon an "altar" cloth. Individual participants frequently bring some personal tools, such as fans.

Christian symbols are apparent in the material structure and paraphernalia, as well as in the prayers and speeches. The tepee's poles represent Jesus Christ and the disciples. The staff is carved with crosses. Sometimes ten carefully selected sticks used to start the fire are regarded as representing the Ten Commandments. Many prayers and songs are directed to Christ by name. The leader sometimes crosses his breast with his hand before lifting the blessed water to his lips in the sacred silver cup. The basic conception, premises, and procedures, however, are native North American, if not specifically Menomini, warped to fit the peculiar needs of the members and penetrated here and there with Christian ideas.

The ultimate declared purpose of taking peyote is to acquire the power with which it has been invested by the Creator (*Kese·maneto·w*). This power cannot be obtained by merely consuming peyote. It comes to one only when the person approaches it in a proper state of humility and after long preoccupation and concentration. If the person is "filled with sin," the medicine will only make him ill, but once Peyote power is acquired, it will enable him to do wondrous things and serves to protect him from evil, including sorcery.

The atmosphere during the first half of the meetings is serious, intense, and quiet. Toward midnight, however, the voices become more emotional and the drumming more rapid. The songs become a cry for help. The prayers become pleas for salvation, for aid and relief from manifest fears, doubts, and guilt feelings. Men pray aloud, give testimonials at certain periods in the ceremony, and frequently break into tears.

Each man seeks his revelations and salvation, and gains power individually. As stated in the ideology, there can be no instruction in the Peyote way; this must come to the individual through his own experience in meetings. Much of this instruction is gained in visions, and some in dreams. However, all members are aided in their striving for revelation, knowledge, and "cleansing of sins" by the efforts of the group in concert—through collective and individual prayers, singing, and drumming and the maintenance of a sacred atmosphere throughout the meeting.

Following are notes drawn from the observations of one of the meetings attended by George and Louise Spindler. Each meeting is different, even in details of ritual (individual leaders and officers introduce minor variations), but all conform to the same general pattern.

We arrived at 7:30 P.M. The members were standing about the yard talking quietly. At 8:45 P.M. the fire tender—a Winnebago from Wisconsin Dells, called us all in. The usual prayer was offered before the door of the tepee (in Menomini) by the chairman of the.night.

After arranging ourselves in the circle of the tepee on blankets laid on fresh cedar over straw, the leader got up to introduce the evening's ritual, state the procedure, and announce the appointment of officials: cedar man (T. B., a Winnebago from Wisconsin Rapids), staff and drum keeper (a Winnebago from Wittenberg), fire tender (a Winnebago from Wisconsin Dells).[5] He also called upon M. to explain the purpose of the meeting. M. arose to do so, saying that the purpose was to "bless the children going off to school."

After this the meeting procedure began with the first passing around of peyote, and the usual singing and drumming, with the drum, rattle, and staff being passed clockwise to each man—who sang four songs.

The meeting was recessed ritually when the drum, and so forth, arrived back at the leader's place about midnight. He preceded his songs by the piping of the eagle-bone whistle—four shrill notes. After his songs were ended water was brought in, cedar was sprinkled on the fire, and the water was blessed by wafting an eagle-feather fan over the incense of the burning cedar and then over the water four times. This blessing was also distributed to the assemblage by shaking the spread feather fan around the circle of participants (this was also done several other times by the fire tender). Then the members stretched out their hands to the fire and made as though to bathe their heads and bodies in its radiance and in the incense of the cedar. The water was then passed in a bucket and each member drank from the silver cup carried by the fire tender, who also served as waiter. The water is regarded as possessing a beneficent power, so one hand is held under the cup to catch any drops. Many of the members laved their faces in some of the water, poured into the palm of the hand.

The meeting was then open for talking. Several men spoke, explaining how they came and thanking M. for putting up the meeting.

Recess was then called and we all went to the yard for about fifteen minutes. We reentered then, and the meeting resumed with a prayer and an announcement by the leader as to procedure for the rest of the evening.

The drumming and singing then proceeded again—two times around the circle—ending at the leader's place with the blessing and cedar incense procedure as before. The "tools" (fans, staff, gourd rattle, drum, and so forth)

---

[5] There are Menomini who can and do fill these offices, but asking qualified visitors to do so is a way of honoring them.

were "smoked" at midnight and at dawn—whenever the cedar incense was burned in the fire and the rest of the blessing procedure had taken place. By then it was dawn (4:30 A.M.) and the water was brought in a second time and the same procedure was followed. Each time the water was brought in it was placed on a cross drawn in the ground before the fireplace and in front of the door of the tepee, and the fire tender, who brought in the water, prayed over it (in Winnebago). This was the only cross used—except for those carved in the staff or represented in the beadwork of the handles of the feather fans.

The meeting was concluded after a third round of singing, at 7:00 A.M., with the ceremonial consumption of fruit, meat, and grain (all wild), brought in by the leader's wife. This was preceded by the usual blessing procedure— "smoking the tools," and piping on the eagle-bone whistle.

The food, consisting of wild rice, venison, and blueberries, was brought in, in large bowls, and placed on a folded mat before the fire. Mrs. R. (the leader's wife) kneeled before it and prayed long—in Menomini. Then the food was passed clockwise, each person taking a spoonful or two. Several took some of the ground venison in their handkerchiefs, to be given in morsels to the members of their families later, as a way of distributing the blessings of the meeting through the blessing given specifically to the food.

When this was finished, the leader announced that the meeting was open to any talks, by any person present who might wish to speak. T. B., D. P., and G. Spindler responded.

After this the leader prayed again, then asked the assemblage to rise together, but pray individually, "each person in his own language," and each one did, conversing with the Creator in familiar terms and asking for blessings for themselves and others. Then the members filed out one by one.

The day following this night was occupied by informal talking, mostly about the meeting and individual experiences during it. A "lunch" of sandwiches and coffee was served in the tepee at 9:00 A.M., and a dinner at 12:40. The persons at the meeting all stayed for dinner and began to leave at 3:00 P.M.

The preceding was a summary of the procedure of one evening. A topical summary of some specific observations, with interpretive notes, follows. They are given in the form in which they were written up in G. Spindler's field notes immediately after a meeting that took place after we had attended several others.

1. Several men cried openly at the meeting. M. cried when he got up to announce the purpose of the meeting. He had just mentioned his father; that he missed him even now, and burst into tears. He continued crying as he spoke. T. B. got up at dawn to speak and cried all the way through his talk. He spoke in Winnebago. The others broke into tears here and there throughout the meeting as they prayed. This overt emotionalism is in striking contrast to anything we have seen in the *metewen* or *ni·mihetwan*. The people in these organizations on the whole exhibit a remarkable composure and constraint both in meetings and outside.

This crying, and the group acceptance of it—the tacit assumption that people will cry, and will unburden themselves—would seem a powerfully attractive factor to people who are seeking some outlet for their frustrations and anxiety, and some acceptance and sympathy.

2. The group support and in-group spirit is an impressive feature of the meetings. The sharing of this long and emotionally laden ceremony, the confessatory atmosphere, all combine to produce a sense of closeness between members that even we, as visiting Whites, felt. One feels loved and accepted.

3. However, despite this "groupness" of feeling, the degree of introversion exhibited is remarkable. Most of the time the men sit cross-legged and stare into the fire (women do not sit in the inner circle). Occasionally, one will get to his knees and bow over, almost touching the ground with his head, and remain in that position for as long as one hour. Men will break into prayer audibly at almost any time—but particularly as a song is being sung. Sometimes three or four people will be praying at once so that there is a low babble of voices. These prayers seem to be triggered by some process internal to the person, and not dependent on the place in the ritual or any specific procedure of the ritual or meeting, as it would be among Whites, or in the *mete·wen* or *ni·mihɛtwan*.

4. The songs sound frequently like a "cry for help." They are sung in a high voice, almost falsetto, with sobs, and a great variation of volume. They sound sometimes as though someone were crying in a minor key and in rhythm with a drum. The singing, the prayers, and speeches all seem to be cries for help, in both content and procedure. This is accompanied by a clear narcissism or egoism in the content of the speeches. Men arise to explain at length just why *they* came to the meetings, what good it did them, and always what trouble *they* had at home, in *their* families, in *their* lives. M. W. spoke of his father, his childhood, his children, and O. P. said, "I don't get around to these meetings very often, but M. came to me while I was up at cherryland and said . . . so . . . I and I. . . ."T. B. gave a long speech about his difficult life and broke down in tears during it. Another Winnebago did much the same. This is in clear contrast to the *ni·mihɛtwan*, where the prayers and speeches are quite impersonal—where one of the "old men" will usually preach, exhort the group as a whole to follow the standards or rules of the drum better, come to meetings more often and so forth, and the prayers are for the group as a whole, at a definite and foreknown place in the ritual, and involve spiritual cognizance of the procedure or sacrifice, or are for some individual who is going on a trip or going to war.

5. I consumed eight peyote buttons during the evening taking two at once and the rest at intervals until 3:00 A.M.[6] I felt slightly nauseated toward the end of this period. I am not sure what other effects I obtained. I did feel,

---

[6] Consumption of peyote varies individually, and the effects vary greatly from time to time and from one individual to another. We observed many people who only ate three or four buttons, a few who took fifteen to twenty, and some who claimed to have eaten fifty or more. Six to fifteen buttons would be, we believe, a modal range for regular members, despite claims to the contrary. Women members eat none at all or (usually) not more than four.

however, very stiff and sore, especially in my lower back, before midnight. This feeling left me after midnight, and I became completely absorbed in the drumming and singing. I tried to let myself "get in the mood," and I seemed to. I felt as though I could sit in any position without moving, for hours, and I did sit cross-legged and immobile for at least two hours in one stretch. I seemed unconscious of my body, though not numb, just detached. It did seem a little like a waking dream state, but I did not sleep, nor did I feel sleepy until about 5:30 A.M. I felt that it would have been easy to drop into a "vision." I did not, possibly because I was so conscious of my role as observer.

The impact of the hours of drumming and repetitious singing, the fire in the center of the tepee, the introverted behavior of the members, and the emotionalism in prayer and speech, all absorb one completely and make one forget discomfort, probably whether one consumes peyote or not.

The drumming seems to contribute to this state as much as the consumption of peyote. The drum is hit very rapidly and quite hard. Each man, as he gets it, shakes water up onto the buckskin cover, then picks up the drum in both hands, places his mouth over the lip of the kettle and onto the drumhead, and blows hard, thus expanding the drumhead by air pressure from inside, the purpose apparently being to make it as taut as possible.[7] Then the drummer begins, pushing his left thumb into the drumhead until he finds a spot where the drum is especially sonorous and at a pitch appropriate to the singing style and the particular voice of a given singer. This pitch may thus be varied as the songs are sung.

The beats are so rapid that there is an almost continuous roll of sound, itself in a minor key. It is literally hypnotic in its effect.

Most of the men who are not drumming will keep the beat with their right hands all night. They may do this by tapping their fans, if they have them, or by shaking gourd rattles, or by merely moving their right hands to the drum's beat. Many of the men seemed quite unaware of the movement of their hands.

Symbolism

The symbolism of the ritual is complex. Each move, each tool, the tepee itself and its structure, have specific meanings.[8] There is variation in these meanings, but there is a fund of common understandings as well. By interpreting the symbolism of the ritual we can see more clearly how Peyotism is the synthesis of Whiteman and Indian beliefs within a native-oriented framework. We have already mentioned the tepee poles, the Peyote Road on the ridge of the half-moon, and the pieces of wood used to start the fire, but there is much more. The

---

[7] The drum chief, it is said, is supposed to do this, but we saw others do it in each meeting we attended.

[8] Slotkin (1952: 580, 581, 586, 587, 643–657) has provided detailed information on symbolism, frequently in the words of informants, that has been essential, in combination with the authors' own observations, to the following analysis.

officers of the meeting themselves represent supernatural forces. The leader guides the members along the Peyote Road as *Kesɛ·maneto·w* guides man along the path of life. He is closely linked with the chief peyote, also representing the Great Spirit, because the latter invested peyote with power. (Sometimes Peyote is thought of as another personified being, or force, but there is considerable variability on this point.) The drum chief sits to the right of the leader and symbolizes Jesus, the cedar man symbolizes the Holy Ghost (*Wayiaskaset awe·tok*, "the one who is a good spirit"), and the fire tender represents the angels (*a·sɛni·wak*, "spirits of the four directions").

These representations seem at first glance to be Christian in origin, but this impression is misleading. *Kesɛ·maneto·w* is not equivalent to the Christian God, even though when Peyotists see him in visions he is often dressed in flowing white robes and has long brown hair and beard (explicitly a Whiteman), for he invests peyote with power which is all-pervasive and resembles much more closely traditional conceptions of power than the Christian conception of grace. *Kesɛ·maneto·w* does not usually punish anyone. However, the Holy Ghost seems to be as much a puzzle to the Peyotists as it is to Christians, and apparently

An altar cloth prepared by one of the members of the Native American Church, with embroidered peyote buttons in the corners and the crown of thorns, the crown and cross and insignia, and the lamb of peace in the center. A staff is being used to hold the cloth straight.

represents good, bright spiritual force closely allied to *Kesɛ·manetoꞏw*, and in contrast to the Bad Spirit (*Maceꞏʔawɛ·tok*). The latter is sometimes called the "Devil" in English, but is actually thought of more as standing for a number of bad spirits who are inimical to man—a conception close to the traditional. The Holy Ghost is also thought of by some as power—that which is invested in Peyote. There is, however, only one explicitly non-Christian spirit in the Peyote pantheon (other than Peyote, himself, a problematic figure in Menomini belief, and the *aꞏsɛni·wak*, who appear ambiguously here and there) and that is the Waterbird, *Aꞏweꞏskenoꞏhsɛh nepeꞏw*, "little bird of the water" (some say it refers to the loon). The Waterbird is often represented in the form into which the ashes of the fire are shaped by dawn by the Fire Chief (though sometimes this figure is said to be a dove) in Peyote jewelry and in carvings of beadwork associated with Peyote tools. The notion of Waterbird is a part of the Peyote complex as it diffused from other tribes, but among the Menomini the idea is fused with that of Thunderbirds, which bring rain that is necessary to life and battle bad spirits.

Some say the half-moon is not necessarily a moon, but a ridge, along the top of which is the Peyote Road. Others say the moon is the light of the night. It guides man through the darkness. All agree that the Peyote Road is the way man must travel, falling neither into the fire on one side nor into the darkness on the other, and that the ritual takes one along the road. In any event, the half-moon altar and ritual is considered (by Menomini Peyotists) to be the "true Indian way" in contrast to the cross-fireplace altar and service used by the Winnebago and others, and at first by the Menomini.

The meanings ascribed to other tools are sometimes ambiguous. Both the eagle-bone whistle and the cedar "incense" (smoke from crumbled dried cedar leaves put in the fire) seem to be forms of notification or communication, linking man and supernatural forces together. The shrill sound of the whistle is heard, by both man and the angels, in the four directions (cardinal points of the compass), or by *Kesɛ·manetoꞏw*, at significant intervals during the service. The cedar smoke rises to the heavens and to *Kesɛ·manetoꞏw* and other powers and is simultaneously smelled by participants. Power is requested and is invested in the smoke, in which the tools, and one's body, may be laved, thus partaking of this power. Some say the smoke takes the prayers of the members with it as it rises to heaven. In any event it does not seem that either the cedar smoke or eagle-bone whistle are Christian in origin, though the ascribed meaning of both appears to include some Christian notions (for example, "angels," and "carrying prayers"). The meaning ascribed to the fan is quite literal. It represents the cooling relief of a fan when one is fevered and ill (or anxious?). The feathers used also represent the Waterbird, which is a beneficent power. The cane is interpreted as support to lean on, literally and figuratively, and to "get to the Almighty" with, or to heaven. The water drum is perceived as an appropriate accompaniment to singing, and possibly does not have other ascribed meanings, but the crisscrossing of the ropes used to tie the buckskin drumhead on forms a star shape which is interpreted by some as the Morning Star, an important deity in traditional belief.

Whatever the Christian elements, the underlying principle seems to be that the specific symbolism is less important than the representation and manipulation of power. All ritual objects and acts, whatever their origin or specific "meaning," participate in power. They both represent power and at the same time bring power to the meeting, to the participants, and into their lives. It is difficult to grasp this principle, for it is cloaked in so many guises. The cedar smoke is important because it carries power. Smoking one's ritual paraphernalia and one's self is a way of acquiring power. The fan is important because it fans, and the fan becomes a metaphor. It "cools," "refreshes," "cures." However, the fan is made of feathers representing the Waterbird, a being with great power, so the fan, used to waft the cedar smoke over other paraphernalia and one's self, participates in, reinforces, and distributes power. The chief peyote is a direct representation of power, and *Kesɛ·maneto·w* is important, not as a stern dispenser of justice, or even of love, but as the origin and bestower of power. Peyote as a medicine must also be understood as power. This medicine does cure the ill, but it is not medicine in the limited Western sense. It is medicine as in a medicine bundle in the old culture. It is the means through which power is concentrated, acquired, and directed. The Peyote Road is not just the path to heaven. Menomini Peyotists are as vague as anyone else about heaven (it is a "bright" place where "good souls" live well forever); it is the path of power that keeps one from disaster. Peyote power is the means to some degree of security and certainty, to survival, avoidance of disaster, curing of ills, to comfort, and to salvation.

With this interpretation it is clear that Menomini Peyotism is more nativistic than Whiteman-Christian in its orientation, however much it is a response to the impact of Whiteman culture. But given the specific expression (for example, Christ and the twelve disciples, angels, and prayers) of Christian elements, it must also be seen as syncretistic—synthesizing elements of both traditional Menomini and Christian belief. This synthesizing helps to make the incongruity between these two systems more manageable for Peyotists. The synthesizing is done within a native-oriented framework. The labels for some objects and events, and the quality of certain limited ideas, such as the images of God and Christ, are Christian. The underlying principle is native. The principle of power and the process of synthesis will be apparent in the personal accounts to follow. These personal statements will show, as no abstract discussion could, what Peyotism means to the participants, and how it functions in the situation created by the confrontation of Menomini and Whiteman culture.

Inspiration and Instruction through the Medicine

There are many patterns of activity and belief associated with Peyotism that are clear carryovers from the traditional culture. Among the more striking manifestations of this are inspiration and instruction. As described in Chapter 2, the Menomini waited for inspiration and even instruction to come to them rather than actively and purposely seeking it out. The *activity* would consist of putting oneself in a position to *receive* the inspiration or instruction. In the first of the two personal documents following, inspiration is not gained by the use of peyote, but the respondent both receives and reproduces the inspiration in the context of Peyotism. In the second case the medicine itself is the direct antecedent to the experience. Both statements make clear what the Peyotist means when he says, "No one can tell you—you have to get in there and learn it for yourself— use the medicine."

Respondent 11

I'll tell you about how I got a song one time. My old aunt that I told you about died. She used me good, gave me clothes, fed me lots of times. I felt bad when she died. I walked way over from W.'s house, he used to live up at Neconish settlement, over to where she used to work. I looked at them things she used to work with. I was sad, standing there and looking at all them things, and thinking about how she used to do.

Then a wind come up. . . . I could hear it up above. I listened to that wind . . . it seemed like it was saying something . . . like it was a song. I listened hard. It was a song in my own language, about her dying. It come right into me, that song. . . . I got it all. Then I walked over to my uncle's house. All the way over there I sung that song over and over, so I wouldn't forget it. I sung it all the way.

I sat down over there, and kept thinking about that. My uncle was watching me. He kind of knew I felt bad because I was so near to my aunt. So he come over and sat down beside me. "Don't feel so bad. We all got to go when our time comes. Then someday we all come together again, be with our friends and all the peoples we knew again." I told him, "I'm alright. I got something real good." So I told him about my song, how it come to me. I sung it for him. "Good! You sing that when we have the funeral meeting." So when we had the meeting next day I waited until just the right time. Then I signaled my uncle, he was leading, that I was ready. So I sung my song, in my own language. Everybody liked it, they thought it was good. It was the first song in Menomini that anybody got.

Respondent 17

One time I was sitting in a meeting. It was on the Fourth of July; we celebrate it that way. Different tribes come in, Winnebago, Potowatami, for a visit. I was sitting there . . . all at once something . . . I could see something going on . . . the last stick, burning on the fire. . . . I see a staff there. I took a good look at it. Everybody was sitting there, but no one else seen what I see. It was made out of a bow, like a bow and arrow. It was like a Thunderbird, with the head here, tail here, and a place to hold it. Just the shape of it like the bow in the shape of a Thunderbird. Just before the meeting was over, the fire went down, and that disappeared. But it looks like something else in there, a few feathers there, like a fan. I see how it's made, for about fifteen seconds I see everything, just how it's made. Just when I got through looking at it . . . it disappeared. It was something given to me. . . . I was supposed to make them tools . . . a drumstick too. . . . I got a drawing of that, everything they use there. . . . I'm supposed to make.

Conversion

Every one of the 15 active male members,[9] during early childhood at least, had experience with a way of life oriented toward the old culture. Seven of them were initiated into the Medicine Lodge, but all of them were raised by comparatively conservative parents or parental surrogates. Every member has also had extensive experience with Western culture. Five have been practicing Catholics.

There are two major trends in these conversion statements. In one, the individual becomes unsure of the meaning of the older religious forms with which he identified and begins to drift away from them. He goes to the Catholic church; he tries being agnostic. For a time he "floats" from one group to another, just as many transitionals do that have not taken up Peyote. However, everything he tries is unsatisfactory—until he finds "a home" in the cult. (Respondent 22 is a particularly good example.)

In the other type of conversion, the individual is, like the first, at a loss as to what to identify himself with. Here, the situation is similar, but the stresses are even more acutely personal. The person has no primary group, no stable friendships, but in the cult he finds security. (Respondent 17 is a clear example.)

In both types, and in all cases, the individual is always marginal and "free floating." He is without secure identifications with any primary groups, and cannot identify with any set of symbols. He has come to doubt the old way of life, but cannot accept Catholicism and the acculturative implications and patterns that go with it. He cannot, however, turn back to the old religious forms or the old way of life. To him, the cohesive, in-group, protective support of the Peyote cult is attractive because it gives him a social body with which to identify and a basis for self-maintenance; and it helps him to resolve the conflict between the internalized patterns of the old way of life and the values and modes of satisfaction of Western culture, for in ritual, premise, and group position in the social structure of the Menomini community, the Peyote cult is a unique combination of the two cultures, even though it is native oriented in principle. Conversion to Peyotism means salvation, both in the literal religious sense, as the convert sees it, and in the broader social psychological sense, as we are speaking of it here. The convert is "saved" from dissolution, self-loss, normlessness, by acceptance of the Peyote way between two cultures. The quotations following, drawn

---

[9] The actual membership of the Menomini Peyote church was always hard to determine since people wax and wane in their interest, and some ostensible "members" never seemed to come to services. The figure 15 represents those males who attended meetings regularly during our fieldwork period. Women are also members, but are much less active in meetings. We estimate a total membership of between 80 and 110, including men, women, and children, but a considerably larger number of Menomini have at one time or another attended services. Active membership has recently (1970) dropped off.

from interviews and conversations with Menomini Peyotists, give meaning to these generalizing statements.

Respondent 22

Some years ago I had an old aunt, sixty-five years old. She got sick, and she was sick a long time, so we took her to the hospital. After awhile the doctor said, "It's no use, she's going to die, no medicine will help her." So we took her home, so she could be comforted in her last hours. The doctor said he would be out with the hearse in two days.

We were sitting around talking when suddenly somebody said, "Those Peyote people, they have a medicine. Go! Talk to them. Tell them about her. Maybe they can help." It happened that they were having a meeting just then. We went over to them. They said "Sure! Bring her over. This is where you Indians belong. This is your place. Not at the other place, here with us." So we took her over, and all that night we sat in the tepee with her. It was a rough go for us. We didn't understand the songs, we didn't understand anything. We took some medicine, to help her, and the others fed it to her all night. The next morning she was still, she was warm. Then later that day we took her home. After a little while she got up! She said she felt good. The next morning the doctor came out, with the hearse just behind. He asked where she was. We told him, "Inside, go see for yourself!" He went in. There she was, preparing breakfast. He stopped. He was surprised so much he could not talk. Then he said, "My God! What happened? What medicine did you give her?" We said "Never mind what medicine. That is the work of the Almighty." He went to his car talking to himself.

That was all I needed. I had been looking for something, somehow, somewhere. This Medicine Lodge was nothing for me. I danced, sung, had a good time, that's all. I was in school. I looked over this Catholic religion. It didn't satisfy me. People go to church, they say prayers, they cross themselves. But it wasn't in here. They didn't feel it in the heart. So I go to some more meetings. I learn more. I listen to them songs. I watch the people pray. Finally I see: "This is where we Indians belong. This is our church."

You know, other Indians and some White men come, tell us we are wrong, that we are crazy. I tell them, "Read the Bible! It tells about Noah. He builded an ark. He worked long. People came to tell him he was crazy. They laughed at him. He kept right on building, him and his little group. Finally one day the others saw that he was right, the great floods did come, and they all ran to his ark."

That is the way it is with us. People tell us we are crazy, that we do wrong. We keep right on, worshiping our own way. We pray how we feel, not the way somebody tells us to. We all pray different, from our own heart.

Respondent 17

Well, I just happen to . . . how I come across Peyote. . . . I was amongst the Winnebago, roaming around after I lost my folks . . . all alone. Of course, I had two sisters, but they in school. I didn't know where to go or what to do, kinda lost like. I come across the people that use that . . . just happened to be traveling through there. Just happened to be a family, very much respected. They invited me to visit them, they asked me how come I roaming around. I told them my bad luck story. I told them I didn't know what to do with myself. Of course, there was other ways I could do . . . drink, carry on like that . . . but I was looking for something good anyway. Of course my Dad didn't know nothing about Peyote. They just told me to watch my step . . . to follow life in a good way. I remember that, what they told me. I had it in my mind. That's what I told them people I visited. They invited me, after I told them everything, they tell me, "You stay with us, you be alright." I was even adopted. "We lost a son, we kind of like to have you," they told me. I kind of made up my mind to help them along . . . whatever they do, cut wood, drive team, take them to town.

They said one time they was going to have a doings. I didn't know nothing about it. They said, "Prayer meeting tomorrow." A big gathering . . . people come from all around. When finally they got started, they told the leader how to run it. . . . I kind of wondered, I was going to find out something . . . how that meeting going to go. The leader talked, "Whenever we have a meeting, there is some purpose; another reason, we got one kind of lost . . . don't know where to go. So I adopt him, make him a son. So we have him join us now." He ask each one to pray for me . . . take care of me as they go along.

That's the first time I use the medicine. I find out about nice people, respectable people. Of course I didn't know nothing about it. I told them about morning, "I think I'm going to follow this, find out for myself, use this medicine . . . follow it up." Then I thanked them. That's all I said. That's how I got started using this medicine, with them people. They used me good. Next morning they was glad to see me . . . they wished me good luck. "Now I have come to something good . . . something . . . very wonderful," I thought. I was glad about it. Until now that's all I have been doing. Now finally they got me to be a chairman and they consider me a very respected man. I never had no trouble of any kind.

Respondent 11

When I was a young fellow I went to these powwow [Dream Dance] and Medicine Lodge. I used to hear all the people say [in the powwow] that the Peyote people was crazy, they carried on all sorts of ways. They said when they took peyote at the meetings they writhed all together on the floor, like snakes.

One time I was at a powwow meeting. Somehow I got to thinking about what they say. So I started walking to where there was a meeting that night. My cousin was there too, and when he sees me going out he caught up and said, "You're going somewhere . . . up there?" I wondered how he knew where I was going. He knew, somehow, that I wanted to see how these peyote eaters looked when they had a meeting; what they did in there. I told him, "I'm going up there to see for myself." So then he said, "Alright, I'll come too." So we went up there together. When we got there it was just about midnight. You know that's when everything really begins at a meeting. Well, we went in and sat down after the intermission. My uncle was there, sitting right across from me. I looked around. Everybody was quiet, praying . . . no one acting crazy or writhing like snakes. . . . I wondered. Then I looked at my cousin . . . he was lookin' around too.

Pretty soon my uncle came over to me. He asked me if I wanted to try some peyote. I said "No". . . . I was scared somehow. Well, we sat there a long time. There was a lot of praying, but everybody was quiet and acted real nice. I didn't see anybody acting crazy. My uncle come over again. He told me, "Come over and sit down by me, at my side." "Alright," so I went over and sat down by him. Then he told me, "I like you nephew. I would like to see you take some peyote. It will do you good, help you. It's up to you though. You can come to the meeting, you don't have to eat peyote . . . think it over." Well, I thought about it, and decided to try some. So I asked my uncle for some. I started eating one, and when my cousin see that, he left. He was scared what was going to happen. Well, I ate just three, like you did the first time. I was scared to try more the first time. Then I sat there, and I felt alright . . . nothing bad happened. Then somebody started drumming and singing. My uncle said to me, "Now listen to this, you can hear something now!" Of course I heard singing before, but now it seemed more loud somehow. I thought, "This is good music. This is better than any I ever heard before." I heard lots of other kinds of music. I sung on the big drum [powwow] many times, and I heard White men's music, bands, and like that, but somehow this seemed more better. I kept listening. I could hear this music way up high, like it was up above my head someplace, coming down from up there. I never hear singing like that before. . . . I kept listening . . . it was something good.

That's the way I got started with the [Native American Church]. I found out who was tellin' all the stories. It wasn't the people in that tepee . . . they wasn't crazy . . . they was alright. I learned something good there . . . so I kept coming back. [Question] I stopped going to the powwow[10] then. I turned away from it. I didn't go back at all until just two years ago. [Question] No, I never go to Medicine Lodge any more, not since I went in there . . . to Peyote, and become a member. This is more interestin', somehow.

Respondent 3

We (G. and L. Spindler) spent the evening with M. and J. B. after a wiener roast in back of their house. M. entertained us with a vivid telling of the story of his conversion to Peyote. Since the telling of it took over two and one-half hours, we cannot reproduce it in his language or with the enormous and significant detail with which he furbished it. We will outline the main elements.

1. He used peyote as a child—at the persuasion of his parents, but when he went off to school, he pulled away from it so that when he returned he tried to persuade his parents against it. One night when his brother J. was

giving a meeting, however, he decided to give it another try. He was curious as to its effects and cynical concerning the experiences he heard recounted by the others.

2. Seated at the meeting, held inside a house, he scorned the four buds the others took, and grabbed a whole handful, eating them "like crackers," to "show 'em" who could eat peyote. His attitude was "know-it-all."

3. Suddenly he heard a voice, "You don't know nothing, nothing at all. You don't even know enough to know where your upper teeth are." Sure enough, when he tried to feel his upper teeth with his tongue, he could not feel them at all.

4. After this, his jaws became weakened, and he was unable to chew the hard peyote any longer, so he called for the waiter and asked him to bring ten peyote all mashed up. He did, and M. was surprised to see that it filled a whole saucer. He was still cocky about his capacity and "knew it all."

5. Then he had his first vision of the evening—a railway depot with a train pulled up to the siding, and a man apparently unloading something, but carrying nothing in his arms. M. was curious to find out what it was he was carrying, and heard a voice telling him, "Take more peyote, that's the only way you'll find out anything. You don't know nothing now."

6. So he continued to take peyote, but he got restive and went outside, feeling somewhat depressed because of his ignorance. He saw angels in billowing, transparent dress.

7. When he returned to the kitchen off the main room, he felt very restless, looked out the window, saw a Western town that slowly changed to a scene in hell, and he could see the horns on the people's heads, and recognized the devil.

8. This frightened him, so he wanted to go in, but someone was singing, so out of respect for him he had to wait. He could not take his eyes off the infernal scene before him.

9. However, he returned finally, took his place, then heard someone clanking chains behind him. He knew it was the devil. He knew it was a message, and that by the Peyote Road he would find salvation.

10. His conversion followed a usual pattern, the contrast of light and dark, evil and good, his abysmal ignorance released only through Peyote. This was interpreted by M. as a lesson in humility.

Visions

Visions are facilitated in Peyotism by consumption of the sacrament, the bud of the cactus *Lophophera williamsii*, which contains nine psychotropic alkaloids, the most significant of which is mescaline, which is hallucinogenic. Considerable research has been done on peyote, mescaline, and, recently, lysergic acid, but confusion about their effects and consternation about their use has not subsided. There is no acceptable evidence to date that indicates that peyote, used as American Indians use it, is habit forming or physically deleterious in its effects.

Vision experiences are almost always a part of conversion, but many visions occur outside of this context. Of all the esoteric aspects of Peyotism, that of visions has received the most attention, and yet there are comparatively few verbatim transcriptions of vision experiences in the readily available literature. Full-blown visions with complete visual imagery are not too frequently experienced. Some of the members stated that they could not remember more than three or four in years of participation. A few claimed they had them nearly every meeting. In all cases they were regarded as events of great significance and were repeated in detail and with care. It is also clear, however, that many psychophysical experiences occur that are not regarded as having such significance. They are usually no more than fleeting impressions, a shape in the fire, a voice, a sound of rushing wind, a sensation of floating, a separation of mind and body.

The content of the "full" vision, involving a definite image, frequently accompanied by audio and kinesthetic sensation, can be categorized under the following headings: instruction and revelation, power-attaining and protection, inspiration, prophesy, and salvation. These categories are not mutually exclusive, and any one vision may express elements from all of them. The theme given greatest significance in accounts of visions is that of salvation, frequently connected with curing, thwarting of the evil power of a witch, or conversion. Contrasts of dark and light, good and evil, hope and despair, with a resolution in the salvation of the sinner through being "pulled up" by the Peyote power, are usually present.

Vision experiences are regarded as sources of instruction, as means of acquiring power, as signs of being "blessed" (having power), as reaffirmation of grace and power attained, as heavenly sanction for one's actions as a sincere Peyotist, as "messages" of importance from the Creator. Visions seem to be "what makes meetings interesting" for many participants. They are something to be "pondered" so that their meaning may become clear. They are also something to be shared with others, as one's experiences during the night-long ritual are discussed in the relaxed social atmosphere of the following Sunday with one's fellow Peyotists.

VISION AND CURING

Respondent 26

One of the old men who started us on Peyote said, "Every meeting something new happens, something different. No one can see it all." Well, he was right, absolutely right. [Do you mean you have different visions every time?] I suppose that's what a Whiteman would say. But these are not visions. They are what you see. Your eyes are open, you're not asleep. It is in your mind's eye you might say, but these things happen because the Holy Spirit from the peyote fills you. The peyote is injected by the word of God with the Holy Spirit. It stands to reason that if you partake of it you are filled with the Spirit. [How do you feel?] Well, if it is a dull meeting, like if it is just a lot of talk about something I'm not interested in, I feel sleepy, relaxed. If it is a lively meeting, like if someone sick has been brought in that we're all working on, I feel full of life, strong. I just want to get in there, trace the illness, do something for the person, use my power to cure with the others.

The peyote works wonders. Your eyes can see what you can't in everyday life. One time my brother was at a meeting. He had been sick, hadn't been feeling good for a long time. I watched him, and I was surprised to see that I could see his bones, just like an X-ray. I kept looking, watching. Pretty soon I could see his organs, all working. I could see his heart beating, his stomach working, everything. I checked up on how everything was working. I watched to see if anything was wrong. But all was fine, ticking along just right. But then I saw a sort of blue spot in his lung, about as big as a man's fist. Then I knew where his disease came from. So I took a button I had in my hand and gave it to him. He ate it. I could see it spread out through his body. It surrounded the blue spot. It pushed it out of his body. It cleaned him out. Soon he was alright again.

You know, this Rorschach [subject was taking the Rorschach at the time] is something like peyote in a way. It looks into your mind. Sees the things that aren't out in the open. It is like that with peyote. At a meeting you get to know a man in a few hours better than you would get to know him in a lifetime otherwise. Everything about him is right there for you to see.

PROPHECY IN VISION

Respondent 5

One time I got sick, then I . . . not much members around Stone Lake, not many singers there, so I want to sing too. They give me forty-four peyote. Pretty soon it started to work. Then pretty soon, I see something. It was a boat, or more a submarine. There was two of them, and one was moving all the time. I don't know what they was. . . . I watched. Then one of them turn over in the water, and you know how it is when something goes down in the water, sinks in the water, there's a whirlpool. Well, I went down in there, I didn't know how far. Sure enough, I feel it, I don't know how far . . . sure enough it come up again. . . . Well, that one what went over, that was the old country . . . that's when the war started, the old country went down, and this country started to shake. That's what I learned that time. Not long after that I seen bombs dropping, and exploding . . . shell holes all around. Then I had my little boy with me . . . carrying him in my arms right through there. I dunno where I'm going but I'm going! I come to a hill, the shells was dropping all around, and I'm going right through. So it seems like it was the war . . . coming.

This was three-four years ago. Somebody was sick. I went over there, but my wife stayed home. I was setting in there, and took twenty or twenty-two pieces, when it got to be morning. All of a sudden I see a vision, a nice room. It had three-four curtains, I never seen them kind before, hanging over each other and split in the middle. One was moving, like somebody was trying to get through. I looked away, and when I look back, the curtains is wide open. I look out, and see the ground boiling, fire coming out, up to about as close as that road over there. I begin to think, I wonder. Then the answers came right in mind. "It's coming close!" That's the answer I got. Now I don't know what that is. Now it seems like this war starting again, and they're going to use this fire . . . [atomic] bombs, you know.

Respondent 5

[How often do you have visions?] Oh Gee! I dunno . . . almost every meeting. Sometimes they come in the morning.

One time I had an experience here at my place.[11] I was kind of sick. My wife told me to boil some tea, so I said, "Well, alright." I put fifty in the little pot, boiled it good, put all that in a dipper, so it was pretty near full. . . . I strained it good when I put it in the dipper. Then when it was cooled just enough so I could drink it I took it down all at one time.

A. and D. come around then, so I asked D. to pray . . . then I took a rest, during the day. When it started to work I was going after water. I could see a real fine wire, like a cobweb, in circles, all even, right up. It seemed like they was going around, I could hear them.

Then I see a Zeppelin . . . big! Then a stool, not exactly a stool, but higher than a chair . . . then a girl, all dressed up. I dunno just what she's gonna do. Then I see another stool, then another young lady . . . both dressed up. This was all inside there, in that Zeppelin. That's the time the boys come over. They brought a drum, and was singing. Then them fan belts, them rings . . . not really fan belts, but shaped like them, some long, some short . . . every time one of them sings one of them fan belts would go off, fly off by itself.

Pretty soon I see a vision . . . the way it looks like in the war. I could see them wheels, all apart, and some stuff burning . . . burning away and smoking. Then I could picture a tavern, and there's a fight going on inside . . . and they was going at it, too! Pretty soon I hear that drum . . . Gee! I feel good! Then I see what looks like police, with blue uniform. He had a box, it looks like a candy box. I see what he's going to do with that . . . he comes to me and says, "Eat that!" I look in and there was peyote in that box. "Eat that in your own home," he says. So that's what I try to do. . . . I put a tepee ground here.

But this other part, it happened that same night, it's hard to explain. It looks like a square jar and it looks like some real fine beads was in there. I could explain that in my own language, but I can't do it so good in English. That's like I explain . . . all kinds of beads, and it looks like water all underneath. It seems like a place in there where there is seats, two of them, with glass in between, going around. It looks like them beads, you gotta catch that in your eye [gestures with forefinger to pupil]. That's what I can't explain . . . how you're supposed to catch that in your eyes. It's supposed to be good for your eyes somehow.

That's what I mean, if anybody was to tell me that, I wouldn't know what they meant. The only way you can find out is to take the medicine yourself.

---

[11] Peyotists frequently use the medicine at home when they are ill.

Peyote himself runs the whole thing . . . no one rank above another. Man power wouldn't work, you got to use peyote. The Almighty gave it to the Indian so we could know there's an Almighty somewheres. You got to pray, ask him the best way you know how. It's like maybe you wash that floor. If it's pretty dirty you need lots of water, if you get a little, it ain't enough. Same way with that peyote . . . you take a little, it does no good. [Question] I take twenty to twenty-five each time. The leader is supposed to take more. The more you take the more interesting it is.

HEAVEN

Respondent 25

[Have any of the people in your church ever seen Heaven?]

Some say they get pretty close. One old man told me how he saw a long stairway, it reached way, way up. There was pretty flowers, real nice, all along the sides. He climbed up these steps, until he got almost to the top. But there was a gate there and two angels, one on each side of the stairway. They were guarding the gate. But they wouldn't let him inside, so he never could see in there. He didn't quite make it. Maybe he didn't live just right.

[What is he—*Kesɛ·maneto·w*—like?]

I see him; I seen him there when I first eat that medicine. . . . He look like White man; tall; well, he's got some kind of white coat on, something like that, like a—I don't know what you call that. [A gown or robe?] Yes, a robe, that's it. I seen that [one] standing there; that's why I like that, this Medicine. . . . he had whiskers on . . . he didn't say nothing to me. I just saw him. [Slotkin 1952:629][12]

EPISODES

Respondent 3

You can always tell when a singer has had a lot of peyote. What you hear before midnight is just warming up. But after that, when the peyote has had its effect, the singing is different. It has a ring to it that it never has no other time. I ain't too much as a singer, but when I think I'm going to sing I take ten to fifteen peyote and keep eating them all night. There ain't many good singers here. Oh, they're alright, but nothing as good as some of the Winnebago. There was two here, they sang small, small. A baby would be bass compared to them. They sang so small, so fine. They ate lots of peyote.

Lots of times I see things that hasn't no story to them, that I know of anyhow. Many times I see these Waterbirds, in the morning, towards the end of the meeting. I even made them fly once. . . . I hollered at them and they all rushed up. I could hear their wings, too.

---

[12] No Peyotist described *Kesɛ·maneto·w* to the Spindlers this explicitly. All three descriptions in Slotkin's texts are of this order.

Then, too, I see a white mass, like the cleanest, whitest snow. It boils and burbles . . . seethes. Every once in awhile it throws up a black thing, that might turn out to be a mink, or an otter, or some other animal. I took that to mean I might have good luck trapping but I never took my traps out to find out.

One time I could see a big field, bigger than that one over there [about ten acres]. That field was covered with deer horns, all over. It seemed like I was looking through deer horns too. Gee! that looked good . . . real nice.

Then once when I started shakin' the rattle I saw a whole flock of wild geese. You know the whirrin' noise they make. I was flyin' with them and could even feel the wind swishing past my wings. They honked and I hollered back at them. Then they would honk again and I hollered again. All the time I was singin' my song with the drum. Then two of the men beside me joined in, but it seemed as if they was always far behind me. I had taken lots more peyote than them. They honked back at the geese, but I was always out in front of 'em. Then my song ended and the geese disappeared.

Another time when I was singin' and shakin' my rattle I saw four corners. It was in a big city and I was standin' on one. Up above me was a big clock in a tower. All the time I was singin' it seemed like my voice would pull the hands a little ways around. I threw my voice up there and hollered and the hands would move. But they would go just so fast. I couldn't make them move no faster. And when the hands had gone clear around my song was finished and the clock was gone.

Sometimes while I was singin' I saw a long, hollow tube that reached way way out. I could holler and could see my voice go down the tube. I would try to throw my voice way down to the other end and then would watch it circle round and round and come back to me. I could do more with my voice than the others because I take more medicine. When the drum stops and I stop singin' the tube goes.

Another time when someone else was drumming, I was way off in that place where people all had that religious dress on, and something around their heads. There was a big tent there and the people were all kneeling and praying and I was praying with them. I could tell it was a foreign land because the air smelled different. I could smell that air so plain! [What sort of a tent was it?] It was a sort of awning-like tent with fringes, sort of khaki color.

HEAVENLY MESSAGE

Respondent 3

I was drumming for J. He was leader that night. I had taken a lot of peyote, maybe seventy of them. When you take a lot you can drum better than the others, you can get all different tones out of the drum. I drummed, and as he began his song I could see all sorts of letters on the top of the drum. As I drummed harder they got bigger, but they kept shimmering so I couldn't read them. I kept trying to get them better and then he finished his song and I stopped drumming and they disappeared. Then he began to sing and I played the drum again. There were the letters . . . all shimmering. They got bigger, so big I couldn't see them, then small, so small I couldn't read them at all . . . when the song got small. I kept trying to get them again so I could see them better, and just when it seemed that I could read them the song ended. I kept thinking, if I had taken more medicine, maybe just four more, I could have read them. The way I see it, it was a message from the Almighty. I cheated my people by not taking more medicine. You always should take as much as you can. If I had taken more I could have read the message and told my people what it was, and given them the word of God.

THE KING'S PALACE

Respondent 3

One time when I was singin' I was inside a beautiful palace, the palace of the King [points above reverently]. There was jewels inside. Such jewels as I never see on this earth. Red, blue, shining jewels sparkling so beautiful. Then there was four men, carrying something between them over their backs [a litter]. It was the King's crown on it. I knew it was because a voice said it was, and it was there on the crown in big letters, "This is the King's crown." They walked to a place in the palace where there was four corners [crosses index fingers to demonstrate]. They stopped there, and it seemed like I was walkin' with them, at the same time and was singin' my song. They turned the crown around and around, and the jewels sparkled. Then I could see the outside of the palace. I could see how big it was. It seemed like I would be both inside and outside it at the same time. Then my song ended and it all disappeared.

Respondent 17

There was one meeting. The leader was praying, when the medicine was working . . . and I was just setting there. This leader enjoyed himself praying. Of course I was sitting pretty close by him. . . . It seemed like I could see clouds on both sides, and a tepee, and we all setting there with our heads down. Seems like this prayer looks pure. Everybody setting around the tepee, all full. And of course there's another part, the caboose. I was listening to the prayer. He was praying for everybody, even for every tribe, even those sick people, even those other Indians doing different ways of worship, even way back to our forefathers . . . the prayer was just pure. The sun coming up . . . it shone in there. It seemed like we all sheep. But we're all Indians . . . all had the blanket on.

On these clouds I could see, it looks nice. It was just like I could see more over there. Seems like the angels was all set on them mountains . . . that's how it looks. Them prayers, all pure. Just then I heard something, like when he is getting through praying, it sounds like "Ph ph ph." I looked around, but everything was quiet. I look at somebody, but nobody else hear that, just myself. I thought they would notice that, but just myself. It seems like them prayers was taken somehow . . . when I hear that noise, hear that floppin'. It went by just like that . . . [snaps fingers]. I didn't ask the others. I studied that. It's just when that leader, his prayers was pure, when I see that. He ain't much of a leader, but much respected. He dunno how, but we all don't know how. Even myself, don't know it all. When I use the medicine, I go right ahead.

The reason for that . . . his prayers was answered, because he was a much respected man, his prayers go straight. That's the way I find out. . . . I just kind of see his prayers go off. That's one of the best. Others I see I didn't study very much. [How often?] I see something almost every time.

IN-GROUP SYMBOLISM

Respondent 11

It's like I was telling you before. . . . I can't hardly tell you much. When you go to the meetings you learn. I learned many things . . . things I was glad, *glad* to know. It comes to you, *somehow* . . . nobody has to tell you, you *know*, you learn yourself, in your own heart.

[Can you give me an example?] I was a good singer, them peoples, they like to hear me sing. I like to sing for them too . . . makes them glad. I learned something about that one time. This meeting . . . I think too much about my singing. . . . I listen to it, try to throw it just right. I didn't think hardly about them other peoples. . . . I didn't think enough about praying with them. Then I was singing . . . it sounded good, I thought. . . . I was singing a song, with my mind on it, and then I see a ring. It was the sound, the song, somehow, right in front of me. It moved around, but I couldn't get into it, somehow. All the others was in it . . . they was praying. But I was left out. Then it moved away, it went, and left me behind. . . . I was scared about that. I told the leader about my trouble. He told me, "Don't worry, you will be alright." He gave me some more medicine, and told me to pray. Then I felt alright again.

PEYOTE POWER

Respondent 3

A visitor who had taken an unusually large amount of peyote spoke at midnight.[13] He arose, put out his hand, and the fan of eagle feathers flew to it. Then he spoke of the twelve disciples, and plucked out each feather from the holder, then cast them to the ground where they stuck upright in a row. When he was through, he put out his hand again, and the twelve feathers flew back

---

[13] This report is paraphrased since, at the time the incident occurred, circumstances prevented its being recorded.

into it. He placed them back in the holder with one motion and released the fan, which flew back into its usual place in front of the chairman.

Another visitor made no speech. He merely got up, took off his shoes and socks, and walked to the fire and stood in the burning coals, saying, "He who believes in Jesus Christ will not burn," then went back to his place and put his shoes and socks back on again.

Protection

Peyotism is a source of protection for the individual in all of its manifestations since it provides insulation against cultural and personal trauma through in-group and symbolic support.

However the protective function of Peyote is more specific than this. The traditional Menomini cultural system provided protection, in the form of ritual precautions, medicines, powerful shamans, and organized associations like the Medicine Lodge, Dream Dance, and, earlier, the Thunder cult, against the machinations of witches and other evil powers. With the disintegration of many of the traditional patterns that could provide this protection, however, and with the acculturating individual's loss of faith in the efficacy of those still available, new sources of protection are needed. Individuals who are still responding to the internalized compulsives of the traditional culture, however much they may be moving away from this culture at the manifest level, are in the situation of being frightened by the old fears and symbols of fears but lacking mechanisms to combat them. The psychological situation is made more precarious by the additional burden of culture conflict, and the self-doubts and generalized anxieties created as individuals attempt to adjust to it. They impute motives to others that may, they believe, result in sorcery, as in one case quoted here. Often those to whom such motives and powers are imputed are members of the native-oriented group, especially elders. Sometimes they are transitional persons, who are even more dangerous, it is believed, because they are not constrained by the norms of the native-oriented group. Sometimes impersonal forces are perceived, like the disease "shape" described by one of the respondents following. The protective function of Peyote is implicit in many of the personal documents preceding. In the three following, this function is made very explicit.

Respondent 4

One time we had a meeting . . . the first part of the second war. There was Indian boys leaving . . . so we had a meeting for them. I had two boys went away. I had a brother, E., went too. We had meeting for them. I was leading. Along about the time when the medicine was affecting my mind . . . I was praying. It seems like I could see wings, tip to tip, down to the earth . . . , covering the earth, and we was all under this. So then, I know, our boys are protected. As I go along, studying about these wings with my prayer, it come to me they was the angel's. Then I turned around, asked the Creator, one of his guardian angels . . . to send one over there, where the war was going on, to watch over our boys. From them wings, it puts me in mind that I should pray to the angels.

That's one experience. Those wings could be eagle's too, represent the American flag. That took place all at one meeting.

Respondent 26

I'll tell you a story that this reminds me of. [The subject was cued to this response by card IV while taking the Rorschach.] Well, first I should say that the old Indian doctors could see sickness like a shadow, as it passed from one person to another. Now there was an old fellow lived back of Zoar. He said one day he saw a shadow coming from a northwest direction, a shape. It went into all the houses, just slapped the people as it went past. But some houses it didn't go into, like B.'s where there was one of our staffs above the door. Sure enough, the next day all those people were sick with deep colds, this phlegm, "h'naek" was bad. All had those colds but the houses it couldn't go into because of the staffs.

Now my girl had a fever. It was high. I was going to call the doctor next day. But I decided to take some peyote. I did, and gave her some. She quieted down, breathed easier. All of a sudden she screamed and jumped at me, and said, "Look! look out the window!" I did, while holding her and there was this thing. It looked like these advertisements with Jack Frost or the West Wind. I saw it there. If he touched her she'd have pneumonia. But I felt sure. I was full of the Holy Spirit. I knew he couldn't touch me, and I told him to go, and he did. Next day she was well and healthy. This thing looked like the disease shape. It has no definite form and is all shadowy.

Respondent 11

In the old times it was different. The doctors, like this *Cese·ko* I was telling you about, could fight the bad men's [witches'] power.[14] But nowadays . . . only protection. . . . I'll tell you. One time I was out working . . . cutting wood, me and my brother. All of a sudden I felt something touch me on the back, and I could hardly straighten up. I couldn't work no more. So I went home. . . . I was in such pain. I lay down but I couldn't rest, and I was weak. Of course I had some medicine, only a few pieces . . . it was scarce then [about 1921]. . . . Well, I took some peyote. I could rest whenever I took that.

Then Thursday [he became ill on Wednesday] I was getting worse. I wasn't suffering, but I was tired, I could hardly move. Well, of course I was brought up to be brave, I could sleep out in the woods alone, never get scared, but I was afraid then. It seemed like every time I took that medicine I could feel something, like somebody was around. I said to my wife, "I believe somebody is trying to hurt me. I been getting along pretty good. Maybe somebody is jealous of me." She said, "Oh? Maybe that could be." That night I was laying

---

[14] The last *Cese·ko* is reputed to have died in 1912, just two years before Peyotism was introduced to the Menomini.

in bed. I took some medicine. I could tell there was something at the door, some animal. I could see the eyes, not clear, but they were lookin' at me through the door. I knew, if I went to sleep . . . it would get me. But that medicine keeps you awake. I kept taking some, every little once in awhile. I set up in bed. If you keeps up they can't get you. If you sleep, he could come in, no matter if the door is locked tight, they got the power to open it, come in, put something in you to kill. Then that thing moved around to the side of the house . . . he knew he couldn't get in yet. I kept watching to see where he was. He come around to the front again. Well . . . all night that kept up . . . him trying to get in. He tried hard, because if they don't get you, they die. Well, it seemed like morning would never come. But next day, whoever it was, he would come, or send somebody to see how I was getting along. They can't move around themselves in daytime, just at night. But next morning lots of people come, I didn't know which one it was that was sent. I was just waitin' for Friday night, they said they was going to put up a meeting for me, all them peoples. So they come, put up the meeting right here in the house. About 11:30 . . . my Dad was singing . . . he wanted me to drum. I was up by then, but somehow I could hardly drum . . . it seemed like my arms was stiff. Then there was two fellows wanted to go home. They was up to Crandon by train to get the medicine night before. They had no sleep, so they wanted to go home, get rest. J. told them, "Don't go now, something going on out there. You might meet him coming up here." But they went out anyway . . . but then they seen a light, like a moon, right by the side of the house, so they run back in, tell my wife and mother, and they run to me and told me "It's come!" So then I was going out . . . meet it face to. But J. say "You stay right here, if he's got the power he can come in!" Then he hand me the staff and rattle. I pass it over to the leader . . . and then, just suddenly, I just slide down right on my back. I couldn't do nothing about it . . . it was like somebody had hold of my legs and just pulled me down. I lay there, I thought, "He's going to get me yet, I think." But then them peoples in there all pray. . . . I could hear them praying for me. And then I felt alright . . . he go away, that one trying to get me.

[Question] we never knew who it was. Somebody die, but it could be any place, maybe far off somewhere. [Question] If that happens to one of the people not in the Peyote way they just have to give up. They try to fight it maybe, but it wouldn't do much good.

Peyote Cures

While visions are a significant and striking aspect of Peyote behavior, the curative function of peyote is probably just as important, or more important to the individual, and visions are frequently seen as simply a part of such curing. To the members "curing" includes not only relief from or elimination of bodily ills but also therapy for despondency and anxiety, a means of absolution of sins, and a process of salvation. These meanings, attached to the notion of "curing," are a part of many of the statements preceding, and are projected, in various combinations, in those following. The curing function, in its various senses, is closely related to the protective function since in traditional belief illness was frequently, if not always, caused by sorcery, or by some supernatural force set in motion by wrongdoing against another person sometime in the past.

If a Peyote doctor is present, the treatment is performed with a ritual that is transparently native in origin. More often, at least with the Menomini, the curing is done simply through the Peyote power and the joint endeavors of the members to influence the supernatural to aid. If the cure works, it is because the individual gave himself sincerely to the absolution of his sins as well as the consumption of peyote. In this usage, peyote is a sacrament. However, it is also regarded as an herb, and is taken or eaten as such. Anything from a common cold to arthritis may be benefited by the peyote thus consumed.

Respondent 4

One time I was working here at Phlox. There was a sawmill at the time. I was working there, on the landing where they haul logs. 12:00 P.M. came . . . time to go to dinner. Then a log fell on me. . . . I couldn't hardly get home . . . took me two hours to go only a little ways. I was sick, hurt. The doctor came, looked me over . . . he want to give me quarantine. I says "No! this is not no sickness. I just got hurt working." So, then, being sick some time, about a month maybe, laying in bed, a bunch of Peyote people come along . . . asked me if they could pray for me. I says "alright" . . . so they did. After the prayer was over they went home . . . then I was alone in the house. Then I could feel something come to me. . . . I know I'm going to pass away. My breath is short, my heart jump. But I have some peyote under my pillow, about fifty pieces. . . . I ate it. No one there to help me. I took water with it. In about one hour, my mind went blank again. Then I was standing . . . like in some basement. I could see all around. Then looking back at me I could see a big chain, like a big logging chain. I didn't know how to get out. Then that quick it come to my mind. "There is a God, somewhere." I say, "Help me!" I could hear something above me . . . it sounded like some person talking . . . can't hardly make it out. But as I go along getting away from them stones. . . . I go higher and higher. It took just so long, then I could see a hole above me. Then there was someone talking in that hole. That voice got closer and closer, as I got up there. As I was getting near this hole, so I could make out who it was. . . . I could tell it was someone praying for me. When I get there, just about to get out. . . . I come to. "Father, Son, and the Holy Ghost," he was praying. Then just that quick I got up. Then I know I'm going to be Peyote member as long as I live. I know there is a God some place. Then I pray, "I be a Peyote member all my life. I try to be good. I never go back to where I was." Then I was well, my body was strong. People was surprised I got up. . . . I was in bed a long time. I could eat a little bit, as I went along. Then, in about another month, I could go back to work. That's one time Peyote helped me. This is my own experience. I was about 22 years old then.

Respondent 3

One time there was a doctor meeting. H. R. was leading it and there was a Winnebago doctor there. After I took a lot of peyote I could see a big operating table, with a body laid out on it. Only the body didn't have no arms or legs. There was a doctor working on it. Then I could hear a voice, coming from above the doctor. This voice was talking, telling the doctor what to do, giving him instructions. But it seemed as though the doctor wasn't listening. The voice, that was God's voice, was telling him what to do, telling him to put the arm where the arm belong, the leg where the leg belong, but the doctor wasn't listening. He had one leg and one arm on the right places, but he was putting the other leg where the arm was supposed to be. Somehow it was made so wherever he touched the body with the leg or arm he was putting on it would stick. He put the leg in the wrong place then, and the body started moving, waving its arm and legs. It wasn't put together right because the doctor didn't listen to his instruction. This is the way I knew the doctoring wasn't going right. It wasn't no criticism of the leader. It was the doctor's fault.

One time I was awful sick—high fever an' everything. I had taken medicine all day long and this night. I was lyin' on the floor watchin' the clock. It said 10:00 and I just kept lookin' at it and thinkin', "I'll be well by morning." It seemed like a long time to wait. Then I seemed to forget everythin'. The next thing I knew I was inside the clock! I could see the gears and the wheels movin' all around me. Then a cat come up and I knew where I was again. The cat arched his back and spat at me. I said, "Boo!" and he jumped inside a bag, then ran up the Christmas tree. I had to go outside. A quarter mile down the road a couple was quarreling. I knew it was a boy and girl without seeing them and could hear everything they saying, clear as could be, a quarter mile away.

The next morning I walked out and coughed up a lot of thick phlegm and was all well. I could even smell the apple trees for the first time, and you know that's hard to do when there are all kinds of trees around and there's no blossoms.

ATTEMPTED CURE AND PROPHETIC NOTIFICATION

Respondent 17

There's another one. . . . I kinda study that once in awhile. One meeting, they doctored a woman, but she died . . . too far gone. This woman was . . . well she and her husband was parted some way, and the woman, she joined the Native American Church, just starting to come in. She had bad luck. Her man was killed along the road, the boys dumped him in the water near Neopit. He was in the water all winter. The very next spring there was this meeting. A Winnebago doctor come, stayed here. . . . I invited him. This woman here, she wanted this Indian doctor to come down, see what he could do. Anyway, he see what he have to do. He didn't have the power to do so, but he's gonna try, ask for power. He didn't quite get started. There was some good reason . . . the Thunderbirds come all of a sudden, and these other kind [Waterbirds], we call them loons, they made all kinds of noise, hollering. At the same time, it was lightning, thundering, close by, all on account of that. They knew right away that woman was in there and they was mad. There was some meaning to all that, and we all in there knew it. Just then, that woman was taken, right after midnight, after we took water. Before she could be doctored she was taken.

A short time after they found that man, some of the fellers in the meeting. Most of them in there knew he was in the water, and two of them found him. It seemed like they was notified in there. There was some noise in there, but I didn't quite get that, somehow. But everybody was talking it over after the meeting, and some of us knew that. I don't know how I could explain that . . . that . . . kind of notified about it.

Respondent 11

I was pretty sick, I had the flu bad. Then I went up to a meeting outside the reservation. I took peyote, and drank some water, and I was awful sick. My head was going around and I couldn't hardly walk. The next day they took care of me, and I stayed at somebody's house. But I didn't want to stay there long. Those people didn't know nothing about peyote, and I wasn't interested in what they talked about. But they paid my fare back. I was still real sick, but I took some more peyote I had in my pocket and I wasn't even hungry. I ate some more peyote while I was at their house, too, and they tried to feed me breakfast but I said I couldn't eat. I didn't want to eat. I went on the bus, and I kept eating peyote to keep me going, somehow. Then I got to the reservation and started walking to where we lived then, not here, over on the other side of the road. I walked awhile, then I got to some old people's house back in the woods. They were all sitting down at a big table, just about to eat. All of a sudden when I saw them I felt like eating. They had everything just like they used to in the old days . . . roast meat, corn, all the same. They asked me to join them. "Alright," I said, so I ate until I was full. Then I went on. "You better run so you get there," they told me. Of course the snow was this [12 inches] deep. So I run all the way. The most times I had to stop was once.

Well, then, I got home. Of course, I lay down, because I was still sick. Then the next day my folks took me to a meeting that was going on. I went in and lay down, J. W. was sitting there too. J. said they should all help me because I was pretty sick. So they give me about thirty peyote all smashed up with warm water so I could take it down good. My uncle told me. "There's nothing we can do for you. The power is all right here. If you want to live, take this." "Well alright," I said. So I took it all down. The water come right back up, but not the rest. Then later they give me thirty more peyote smashed the same way. I took it all down. Sometimes, too, I take some dry peyote, about fifteen, in there.

Well, I was lying there. My head was turning . . . dizzy. Then they were singing. . . . I listened to that. Then all of a sudden I see a big stairway in front of me. The first step was right like this [points out weathered stoop] right by me. It seemed like them steps was all glassy. They was shining, real nice, gee! they was clean and nice. The first was about like this here [indicates porch stoop again], . . . and each one got brighter it seemed like, all the way up. I could see them all, one by one. Up to the top it seemed all bright and light, real good, clear. Then I knew I would be well next day. The next day, sure enough, when I woke up, I felt good.

[What did those steps mean?] Well, it seems like to me it means that if I keeps on living good, and learning more and more, I could climb them steps one by one, somehow. That was the first time I ever see anything at a Peyote meeting.

Respondent 11

The Peyote doctors is all south. Them people going at this a long time.
[How do they work?]

Like them other people. Somebody get hurt, or some kind of a sickness, they go out to different doctors, maybe they never get cured. So they come back . . . try Peyote doctors. About the last thing they can try. These doctors has different ways. One doctor, he use a silk handkerchief . . . hold up handkerchief, look at person through that handkerchief, then put it away. I never seen this, but I heard of it. Some use whistle, blow on person, all over. Then they use three long yellow feathers, they're sharp on the end. They pick that sick person, they suffer, but they hit that right spot. They know it then. In their fireplace, the coals is red hot. They go over there, pick up coals, put it in their mouth. I seen that, they done it right here. They blow it in the sick person . . . red hot after they get through, they throw it in the fire again. They go over there, suck that sickness right out. Whenever he get through he get up, go over, spit that right in fire. Oh, they do that maybe four times, they do that all meeting. The next morning, first thing, them people be up. That's the way them doctors do it.

AN UNSUCCESSFUL ATTEMPT

Respondent 4

One time we had a meeting here. There used to be a house then, where that apple tree is. They tell me a White man is coming—paralyzed for ten years —been all over the country. We got together and put up a meeting. Along toward evening they brought him and his wife. We put the man on a bed and his wife alongside of him. I was the drummer for the leader. He says, "Fix up medicine for this man. Fix some medicine for him and some tea." So we did. We fixed up one-hundred pieces, ground it up, gave it to him. We pray for him, the singing was going around, different ones singing. Along about midnight this man sat up on his bed, and he swung his legs down towards the floor, and one of his feet was moving, just like the drum was going, keeping time. So we give him some more. And this woman was beginning to get scared. She thought this man was going crazy, and this woman said, "Don't give him any more." About that time it was getting along towards morning. As the quitting time came, the man was still sitting up, but didn't walk yet. And this lady wanted to go right away. Because this man was under the peyote we told them not to go. But this lady got help somewhere and got this man out. That's the last we saw that man. He promised he'd come back. . . . He never came back. That's one explanation we had at the meeting. If he had taken more peyote, he could have walked, which he never did for ten years.

The personal statements just presented have provided us with an experiential view of Peyotism. We have interpreted those statements functionally, showing how the Peyote experience helps resolve culture conflict, provides a primary group and security, cures ills, and protects against witchcraft and other evil influences through power. It remains for us now to explore the consequences of commitment to Peyotism in the psychological organization of individuals, and the nature of Peyotism as a social movement.

Peyotism and Psychological Process

Conversion to Peyotism is an intense emotional experience; a resolution of doubt and conflict. This experience, the ritual, the close in-group feeling, and the presence of hallucinogens in the sacrament suggest the question: What are the Peyotists like psychologically? Menomini Peyotism seems to be native oriented in principle, yet syncretistic in many dimensions. Are the Peyotists psychologically similar to the members of the native-oriented group? Peyotists are also people who have experienced culture conflict as personal trauma and who have come to doubt themselves as they have interpreted these conflicts and traumas. Most were in a transitional state before they became Peyotists, even though most were raised in traditional households.[15] Has this transitional experience had any effect on the psychology of the members? Peyotism is an adaptive response to confrontation. We have described this strategy in its social and cultural dimensions. What are the psychological concomitants of this adaptation?

Questions of this sort are never easy to answer. It is not even simple to decide what is meant by "psychological." We have described the ritual of Peyotism, the behavior of Peyotists, and have provided samples of the personal experiences and interpretations of those experiences by members. Are not all of these dimensions, particularly the last, psychological? In a sense they surely are. All of them may be treated analytically to render inferences relevant to the perceptual, cognitive, and emotional organization characterizing individuals, or the shared attitudes and motivations of members of the group.

The difficulty with doing this is that the process of analysis becomes circular—one infers from known behaviors to a construct called "personality" and then

[15] All of the fifteen males studied as individuals in our sample were raised in traditional households, but some marginal participants were not.

says, "See how it fits!" Some of the earlier personality and culture work in anthropology made this error. What strategy can be adopted to avoid it? One way would be to separate very clearly what is normative and ordered in the Peyote ritual from the reactions of individuals to it. The kind of material we have included in this chapter would make this possible, and to some extent we have done this, at least implicitly. Yet there is a problem. Menomini Peyotists introduce considerable variability into their ritual, and they participate so wholly as individuals in the ritual setting that it is very difficult to separate one from the other. Another strategy would be to use autobiographies as sources for psychologically relevant inference, and direct observation of behavior as a source of inferences concerning culture. We have used biographical material in this way, and it is useful but difficult to standardize.

Our solution, as stated in Chapter 2, was to use the Rorschach. This device provided us with culturally ambiguous but standardized stimuli—the same ten inkblots were administered in the same order to each person in the sample. Individuals responded to the inkblots with various perceptions as they answered the questions—What do they look like to you? What do you see in the blot that makes you think of that?—This variability is in part a product of differences in the psychological characteristics of respondents. We say "in part" because there are intervening factors. No two administrations, even by the same administrator, are exactly the same. The situation of administration also varies. The immediate pressures upon the respondent vary. Suggestibility and subliminal cueing by the administrator may also be factors. These intervening factors, and the known variability of response to the Rorschach at different times by the same individual under repeat test conditions, inclines us to discount the significance of individual protocols as adequate representations of total individual personalities. What we are interested in is modalities and ranges in perceptual-cognitive and emotional organization within certain population samples. We have five acculturative-adaptive groups in the Menomini population, of which the Peyote group is one. Each of these has been sampled with the Rorschach and a sociocultural index schedule.[16] The differences between samples in both of these dimensions, as shown by chi-square or exact probability tests, are of interest. We will not be able to explore the intricacies of this analysis and its results in this volume. Those readers interested may read the more technical monographs and papers in the "References" and the chapter on fieldwork methods used with the Menomini in *Being an Anthropologist* (G. Spindler and L. Spindler 1970). Some of the major results of the analysis are relevant in this case study, particularly where the Peyotists are concerned, and we will discuss them now.

The Peyotists are highly deviant within the Menomini sample. Their Rorschach responses differentiate them consistently from every other acculturative category, and they are internally (as a group) homogeneous. Only the native-

[16] This schedule consists of twenty-four items, such as knowledge of the Menomini language, display of native objects, membership in religious groups, type of furniture in the home, condition of the home, and so forth, that were considered to be denotative of acculturative and socioeconomic status. A schedule was collected for every male (sixty-eight), female (sixty-one), and member of the White control group (twelve) in our whole sample. The schedule is available in G. Spindler, 1955, and L. Spindler, 1962.

oriented group is as frequently differentiated from other groups. The Peyote group is, however, distinguished from all other groups in different ways than is the native-oriented group. We will concentrate now on these particular attributes.

The Rorschach responses of the Peyotists are distingished from those of all other groups in the proportion of responses concerned with human movement (for example, "There's a person walking up that trail, up towards this other crowd up here"). It is also the only group in the sample that consistently exhibits a predominance of such responses as compared to animal movement responses (for example, "That looks like a bear scratching on a tree trunk"). The Peyotists also produce responses that are scored for diffuseness as a prevailing characteristic more frequently than any other group in the sample (for example, "All this part here is smoke"). Likewise, they produce more responses that require three-dimensional views of the two-dimensional inkblots (as all flat "pictures" are) (for example, "There's a tepee way back in there, and a path to it from here, with these rocks on the sides"). They also show some signs of what is regarded as looseness in perception of structural forms—their responses sometimes disregard obvious features of the outlines and relationships among different parts of the inkblots. They exhibit strong differentiation in responses to color (for example, "Here's a big explosion, all fiery"), with color dominating other possible qualities, particularly the form or outline of the blot as they see it. In these last two indexes the Peyotists are not distinctive from the transitionals.

It is true that even the most modest interpretations of the psychological meaning of these indexes raises questions of validity. We apply two analytical strategies to this problem, though neither solves it completely. The first is to take account of the fact that the deviation of the Peyotists' scores in comparison to the other acculturative groups and without regard for specific psychological meanings, is indicative of a psychological[17] position for the Peyotists. The Rorschach responses are separate data, separate from direct observations, verbatim accounts of experiences, reports of ritual, expressive autobiographies, and information about symbolism. We may use these responses in a comparative framework provided by the universe we are studying—the Menomini—to define psychological similarity or difference between the various groups in our sample of that universe. On this basis we can, for instance, say that the Peyotists are more different psychologically from the native-oriented and transitionals than they are socioculturally (on the basis of data from the sociocultural index schedule), for they show far more Rorschach differences than they do sociocultural differences. We can say that the Peyotists are psychologically more like the transitionals than they are like the native oriented. We can make the statement that the transitionals, who, unlike the Peyotists, have no single primary group to which they belong, do not exhibit the same degree of deviation from the rest of the sample as do the Peyotists and are not as interally homogeneous. Some of our questions are already answered.

The second strategy is to apply the most modest interpretations we can to the Rorschach indexes that differentiate Peyotists from others, and then see if these interpretations fit Peyote ritual and symbolism, ideology, and behavior.

---

[17] By "psychological" we refer to perceptual structuring, cognitive process, and emotional expressiveness and control as being what is displayed in Rorschach responses, but without, at this stage of analysis, inferring specific characteristic from Rorschach scores.

We have distinguished six critical Rorschach differences between the Peyotists and the rest of the Menomini. The first two (percent of human movement responses and predominance of human over animal responses) may be considered together as indicating an unusually high degree of concern with the human world, as against the animal or object world. If we look at the human movement responses of the Peyotists, we find that there is frequently a tendency toward concern for motivations and feelings. "Right here, it looks like two people here. They kinda join hands together. Seems like it makes these dark clouds up here light up, like if those two people did join hands, them clouds would disappear. Like if they understood each other . . . they're gettin' mighty close to it . . . the light is comin' down." Many responses, however, are straightforward humans-in-action percepts such as, "Looks like a couple of people up there, pulling up a pail." We can say that the Peyotists exhibit a high degree of interest in human behavior, with some direct evidence of concern with motivations.

If we look at behavior and statements about behavior in the context of Peyote meetings and the Peyote ideology, we find strong evidence that Peyotists are concerned with themselves as well as with others. They are concerned with their own past, the things they have done wrong, and their redemption. They are concerned with acquiring power so that they can travel the Peyote Road and thwart evil. There is intense self-concern, and this is reinforced by the Peyote ritual and setting, as described previously. The mescaline in the peyote also has the effect of turning one in upon oneself, at least in this ritual context, aided by the hypnotic drumming and singing, staring at the chief peyote or into the fire, and being surrounded by others praying in their various private ways to *Kese·maneto·w*. It is plausible to infer that the deviant concern with human movement in Peyotists' Rorschachs reflects all these dimensions of the Peyote experience.

The responses scored for diffuseness are usually regarded as indicative of free-floating anxiety. This kind of response is virtually absent among the native oriented, frequently present among the Peyotists, and only occasionally present among others in the sample. There is ample evidence of anxiety in the statements and behaviors of Peyotists. One may say that the reason most Peyotists are Peyotists is because of anxiety. It is projected in a number of specific concerns, but is a pervasive process in individual adjustment. They are anxious about their identity, belonging somewhere, "doing right," the threat of witchcraft, their health, losing their lands to the Whiteman, and salvation. These anxieties are clear in the records included in this chapter.

The Peyotists' Rorschachs also include a deviantly large number of three-dimensional responses. These are usually interpreted as suggesting tendencies toward introspection. Such an interpretation is compatible with what we know of Peyotist behavior, rationale for behavior, and ideology. The ideology specifically sanctions introspection, aided by the medicine, as a means to knowledge and power. Much of the behavior at meetings is introspective in nature. It seems closely related to the self-projective fantasy suggested by the preponderance of human movement responses. Here again, there seems to be a strong relationship between the Peyote experience and the psychological characteristics of Peyotists as inferred from Rorschach responses.

The remaining two Rorschach indexes may be considered together—the tendency for color to dominate other qualities in Peyotist responses (when bright color is present in the inkblots) and the tendency toward looseness in perception of structural forms. The first may be interpreted as suggesting less controlled emotional responsiveness (than in form dominated color), and the second as a looseness of control in the perception of ordinary reality. The relative looseness in emotional control seems supported by behavior in meetings. For example, crying when praying or speaking seems not only to be sanctioned but virtually required. It is a way of expressing sincerity. This tendency has been noted by others who have worked with Peyotists. It is in such sharp contrast to the controlled composure of the native oriented that it is, together with introspective rumination, the earmark of the Peyotists' adjustment. The possible looseness in intellectual, or reality control, is more problematic. It is a logical but not necessary corollary of looseness in emotional control. There are no specific concomitants in behavior or ideology, and, if anything, Peyotists appear to have the rationale for their ritual worked out better than the native oriented. Perhaps Peyotists become less concerned with "ordinary" reality as they become more concerned with "nonordinary reality",[18] or is it a product of unresolved conflict? At present we have no good answers to these questions. In any event looseness in perception of ordinary reality is not incompatible with the complex of psychological characteristics and relevant behaviors and sanctions for behavior that has been developed in this discussion. To be sure, this "looseness" in no way seems to handicap the Peyotists in making a living or getting along in their daily affairs. We conclude that ruminative, self-projective concern, introspection, diffuse anxiety, relative looseness of affect control, and possibly looseness in the perception of ordinary reality are the distinguishing psychological features of Peyotists. Our conclusion is based, as the preceding analysis should show, on statistically compared Rorschach indexes, knowledge of the Peyote experience, and information concerning individual adaptation.

We are left with another question, however. We have some understanding of the distinctive psychological features of Peyotists. What caused them? Causality is also a slippery area when dealing with human behavior. We can identify concomitant relationships, but these may often turn out to be fortuitous, or the result of convergence that only appears to be causally related. Is the apparent interdependency of these psychological features and the Peyote experience fortuitous? If the Peyote sample consisted merely of people from the much larger population of transitionals without any special relationship between psychological features and Peyotism, we would expect to see a random distribution of the same features in this transitional population that are distinctive for the Peyote sample. Some of the features are present among transitionals. The Peyotists are not clearly distinguished from the transitionals in emotional and reality control. There is some experience that both Peyotists and transitionals have shared, we infer, that produced similar psychological adaptations in both. However, the Peyotists are clearly distinctive from the transitionals in the predominance of concern with the human over the animal and object world, amount of diffuse anxiety, and introspective tendencies. The Peyote personality syndrome, as we have described it, is not found in its complete form among the transitionals insofar as our sample reveals. This

---

[18] We owe these terms to Carlos Castenada (1968).

is all the more remarkable in that about one-half of our transitional sample at one time or another had experience with Peyotism. Apparently, for them Peyotism was a temporary way station on the road to a more acculturated status. The fifteen males in our sample have, in contrast, found a "home" in Peyotism.

It is important, however, that the transitionals and the Peyotists do share some psychological features, and particularly important that in their sharing of them they are together distinctive from either the acculturated or the native-oriented group. That is, looseness of affect and reality control are distinctive features of both Peyotists and transitionals. These features are what one might expect among people who have lost faith in traditional cultural norms for behavior, who don't think that the culture of their parents and grandparents works any more. The transitionals have not found or created a new culture or (in some cases) are just in the process of doing so. The committed Peyotists have found one, and, in fact, helped create it out of the materials at hand. They became so closely identified with it that they and their culture seem inseparable. Their present psychological adaptation is the result of this close interdependency. Does Peyotism cause this characteristic adaptation? In the sense of this interdependency it does.

Recruitment

Recruitment into Peyotism, among the Menomini, can be described as fortuitous, within a broad structurally conducive base. (These are formidable terms, but they have their advantages.) The relationship between psychology and experience in the Peyote church that we have discussed is not fortuitous, but recruitment seems to be. The way in which Peyotism came to the Menomini in 1914 is instructive. Before that time several families had split off from the conservative Zoar faction and had moved into the northwestern part of the Menomini lands into what became known as Neconish settlement. They had moved up there, it appears, because they were dissatisfied with the nature and conduct of the traditional metɛ·wen, and with the ni·mihɛ·twan, which was then still a "new" religion itself, having arrived about 1879. They were ready for a change. Along came Mitchell Ne·kwatwe·h, the Potowatomi Peyote missionary, to live with the Neconish family to which he was related. The oldest Neconish son took up Peyote right away. The others followed soon after. A nucleus of Menomini Peyotists had been created. About this same time the last of the shamans were dying off, the powers of the traditional organizations were declining along with the organizations, the medicine bundles were being burned or sold off to museums, and the flu epidemic was wiping out the elders who were the carriers of esoteric knowledge and power. Lumbering operations, schooling, religious proselytizing, diminishment of game and fish as subsistence resources were bringing the traditional Menomini culture system to its knees. A "broad structurally conducive base" was being created—conducive to the emergence of a religious movement. On the Plains the first major movement of this kind was the Ghost Dance, which resulted in the massacre of Wounded Knee, where the White military authorities panicked at the prospect of more Indian wars. There had been other movements before that on the Plains, but none so sweeping, and there had been a number of others in the central forest area, beginning shortly after contact. Among the Menomini Peyotism got off to a good start. It was a redemptive movement, providing a means of personal salvation, and not a transformative or revolutionary movement aimed at changing the world (or even the Agency), so it appealed to the Menomini, who were not particularly aggressive, and who would have seen a challenge to Whiteman authority as hopeless. The nucleus of enthusiasts at Neconish settlement proselyted effectively. There were people everywhere who were "looking for something, somewhere," and who found the weakening traditional religious forms unsatisfactory, or perhaps even dangerous (power, if not controlled properly, can cause unpredictable damage), and who found the tepee a good place to be. However, there was no planned proselyting, and whoever happened to come to the meetings was welcome. Menomini move about, as most Indians do, almost constantly. They go to see relatives, change residence seasonally, establish contacts here and there. A number of people in a ready state met up with members of the nucleus or heard about the new religion, so recognizably and explicitly claimed as Indian ("this is where we belong"), and came to meetings. Some stayed, others did not. Enough stayed to keep it going, though Peyotism never took hold with the Menomini as it did with most Plains tribes, and as it has taken hold with the Navajo recently.[19]

The coming of Mitchell Ne·kwatwe·h to Neconish settlement was fortuitous—he happened to be related, and the people there happened to be ready for him. It was the right time for this to happen. Peyotism would not have happened in the 17th century, when the traditional religious forms were in full force. After the nucleus of Peyotists was established the incorporation of new members was fortuitous also—in the manner just described. Selections of new membership occurred non-fortuitously only in that those who stayed (as opposed to those who came but did not stay) may have been those who were more marginal, more isolated, more psychologically ready. The Peyotists and the transitionals, we infer, are from the same category of dispossessed. The difference between them is the Peyote experience.

Once the neophyte begins to go to meetings, he begins to become a Peyotist. His commitment is deepened by exposure to the Peyote ideology, communicated in many different ways by older members; by the experience of conversion, with its dramatic emotional overtones and its resolution of conflict and doubt; and by traveling the Road in meeting after meeting. The people in the Peyote church, or coming into it, are people who are anxious about their fate. They are in a psychologically ready state. They need conflict resolution. They need to find reassurance that they are on the right "road." They need an identity. They need to

[19] David Aberle's excellent analysis of Navajo Peyotism (1968) presents the case for "relative deprivation" as the antecedent factor among the Navaho. He uses the Menomini data comparatively to show how Menomini Peyotism was an acculturative-transitional process, in contrast to the Navajo situation. We accept his analysis but think that it is clear that "deprivation" in the broad sense of being deprived of security and identity as well as livelihood and lands is the conducive base among the Menomini, but that fortuitous selection accounts for the actual membership. The fact that a large and undetermined (virtually undeterminable) number of Menomini transitionals have had Peyote experience (in our transitional sample, about 50 percent) indicates that for some, perhaps the majority of those who have contact with Peyotism, it serves as an acculturative-transitional experience. Only the core members appear to represent the psychological features described.

be rescued from despair and loss of self-control and self-respect. As they see it, they must be cleansed of sin by the power of peyote. In this sense they need "redemption." As they are redeemed, their organization of emotions and of cognition and perception become, we hypothesize, virtual projections of the ritual, symbolism, and ideology of Peyotism. The unity of culture and of individual psychological organization is apparent.

When we look at the total relationship between Peyote experience and Peyote psychology, we are led to the inference that the peyote itself and the mescaline it contains are almost incidental. What is important is the existence of a tight-knit, responsive, supportive primary group, an organized system of meanings that is dramatized again and again at every meeting, and the fact that these meanings are in themselves a dramatization of the dilemma of the uprooted human. The Peyote Road is the path to salvation and redemption, but salvation is a metaphor for a satisfactory, secure, and knowable way of life. The Road itself is the trail between fire and darkness, but fire and darkness are metaphors for an unknowable past and an uncertain future. The Peyote church is a kind of semipermanent "encounter"[20] session where the deepest secrets and feelings can be bared in the company of others, and where the usual norms concerning control and independence are dispensed with. Peyote meetings are more effective than most encounter sessions, however, because Peyotism has an internally consistent culture of its own that can be acquired by the seeker and, once acquired, continues to solve problems. The peyote is important as a sacrament, which is needed in sacred rituals. The visions are important as an experience insofar as they relate to the content and symbolism of Peyotism, and most do, but most members have them only infrequently, and some of the most devoted members very rarely have them. The feelings of detachment, the ability to concentrate on the songs, the drumming, the fire, the Peyote Chief, which are enhanced by the consumption of peyote, are important, but detachment and concentration are common human features of intense religious experience with or without the aid of hallucinogens. The peyote does provide a rationale—learn from peyote, no one can teach you— that is important as a path to insight and revelation in any context. It also provides a sense of daring the unknown that may be important in conversion. To use Leon Festinger's now classic term, one experiences "cognitive dissonance" about the taking of peyote (Festinger 1957). It is dangerous, one has heard. It makes a person who has sinned very much quite ill. It may put him out of his head. However, he goes to a meeting, and friendly people there urge him to take peyote: "You can only learn what this is all about if you do." He takes it. He experiences great relief. He is not dying, and he did not get *very* sick, or if he got sick, he got over it. When the dissonance is resolved, he immediately looks for ways to defend himself against any doubts concerning the wisdom of the choice made. The Peyote way becomes the only way.

The process of recruitment discussed gives us an understanding of the appeal of Peyotism to some of the now middle-aged or older generation of Menomini, close as these particular individuals were to the native-oriented way of life in early

---

[20] Meetings, common in California and known elsewhere in urban America, where mostly middle-class people try to become less defensive about their feelings and self-other appraisals.

childhood, but growing up doubting its efficacy. It also suggests that for the present younger generation Peyotism will exert less appeal. Few people under twenty-five in the present population have had much experience with a native-oriented way of life. Their struggle is not so much for a resolution of culture conflict. They have already been robbed of their traditional culture by the long-term processes resulting from the confrontation we have described. They are struggling, if at all, for recognition and identity in a kind of social and cultural no-man's-land. Some form of radical political activism is more likely to prove attractive. As we have said, however, the significance of Peyotism for understanding what has happened in many other American Indian populations, as well as the Menomini, over a relatively long period of time while the traditional cultures have still exerted substantial influence, is very great.

There are also many parallels to Peyotism among the non-Indian American population in, for example, psychedelicism, and in the proliferation of neoreligious groups among college students and others, some of which provide a cognitive-cultural synthesis of certain features of Eastern and Western belief. Many other movements in contemporary United States society exhibit some of the attributes of Peyotism, including utopian-communal movements and various countercultures, as well as marijuana smoking, when it is ritualized as a communal event.

The Peyote Women

The Peyote way becomes the only way for the committed member. Most committed members are males. Women among the Menomini have the right to participate in the ritual, though this was not always the case, but most of the women are much less involved than are their husbands or fathers. No offices are held by women. A woman, usually called the "dawn woman," sometimes the wife of the leader of the meeting, sometimes the sponsor's wife, brings in the ceremonial breakfast, and often the water. Occasionally, this woman, or some other, if the spirit moves her, will pray, as does the leader, for the assemblage as a whole. More often she will merely speak, welcoming the guests and inviting them to come to the meals to be served the next day. The female members of the sponsor's family, and other volunteers, help prepare these meals, frequently during the night while the ritual is taking place. When the women do come to meetings, they lie behind the men, where they not infrequently sleep, and in any event, block the cold draft, whistling under the edges of the tepee, from the men's backs. Some women, particularly the younger ones, take no peyote or only consume one or two buttons. Some drink peyote tea, or eat some of the ground and moistened peyote as it is passed around in the earlier part of the meeting. Few have visions.

The women do, however, not infrequently make secular use of the peyote in a practical manner. As one woman said:

> One time I was gonna make a pillowcover. That time I took forty pieces of medicine, wonderin' how I was gonna get my pattern. My husband took me to Antigo and just past the reservation line I saw a thunderstorm coming. While I was starin' at the sky I could see a blacker cloud above us. This cloud gradually

One of the leaders of the Native American Church and his wife.

formed the shape of a bird and how it looked. It looked as if the cloud turned into a bird. So I could tell just how. I took them for a pattern. They say if you want a rainbow, just take enough medicine.

Later she said:

When my youngest girl was about a year old, she got real sick and her fever went way up and we thought she was gonna die. While she was lying there she kept pointin' up at the cupboard. Then I saw she was pointin' at the pitcher where I always keep some tea [peyote]. So I gave her some and some more later. Soon she was sweatin' good and by morning her fever was gone.

The last time I went to the hospital to have my baby I took a bunch—about nineteen buttons before I went, and told D. to pray for me, and I got along fine. They didn't give no drugs then, so it helped me. (Menomini woman, in L. Spindler, field notes).

In view of the lesser commitment of the women to the ideology and sacred practice of Peyotism, do the women exhibit the same perceptual organization as the men? The strongly introspective and self-conscious rumination characteristic of the men is not as strongly developed among the women, who are more outward oriented. The women also exhibit somewhat more control over emotions than do the males, and seem to be somewhat less anxious. In general we can say that the women exhibit diminished Peyote psychological characteristics. This is what we might expect, given their lesser identification with Peyotism. The Peyote women are, however, like the men, psychologically deviant within the Menomini sample of females from all acculturative categories.[21] Some of the same processes probably operate in the recruitment of women to Peyotism as for the men, but since it is almost entirely women married to Peyote men, or their daughters, who are members, this process is not as clear-cut. The deviation they do present may be the result of their participation in the ritual, symbolic process, and ideology, even though this participation is relatively limited.

Conclusion

In this chapter we have described and interpreted one of the adaptive strategies some of the Menomini have utilized as they have coped with the confrontation between their culture and Whiteman culture. We see Peyotism as a syncretistic movement with redemptive overtones eliciting a high degree of commitment from fully participating members. It is syncretistic because it combines and rationalizes beliefs, symbols, and behavior from divergent cultures and redemptive because it reduces self-doubt and provides an acceptable identity for those who have lost their way. It is not transformative. It does not seek to change the world. It redeems the individual whose self and self-respect have been eroded by the loss of cultural norms and values and by the loss of the support of a stable ingroup. We have analyzed recruitment into the movement as fortuitous within a broadly conducive structural base. We have tried to show how the ideology, ritual, and symbolism are a synthesis within a native-oriented framework of cultural elements from both Menomini (and broadly Indian) and Western culture, however discongruent these two cultures are. Menomini Peyotism, both as a religious-redemptive movement and as a synthesis of discongruent cultural elements, is functional in the adaptive process.[22] It is a microcosmic expression of the conflict between cultures, and of one kind of solution, widespread elsewhere in this world of cataclysmic change, to the dilemma that the native oriented solved another way.

Now we turn to the much larger body of transitionals, to the people who have no ritual, no consistent ideology, and no tight-knit primary group identification but whose problems are the same as those faced by the Peyotists. How do they adapt?

---

[21] Those who wish to pursue further the Menomini male/female differences in roles, values, and Rorschachs might read *Menomini Women and Culture Change* (L. Spindler 1962) and "Male and Female Adaptations in Culture Change," L. Spindler and G. Spindler 1958).

[22] Students wishing bibliographic references on various kinds of religious and neo-religious movements will find "Material for a History of Studies of Crisis Cults: A Bibliographic Essay," (LaBarre 1970) very useful.

4

Those In-between

I don't know where I belong. I don't go to church and I use Indian cures for different things. . . . I can't go to church now. If I should die I suppose I would be buried out in that potter's field. [Transitional Menomini woman, age 40]

THE IN-BETWEENERS are Menomini with acute problems of identity. They have had experience with the native-oriented way of life, and many of them have been baptized, though most are (to use their own term) "lukewarm" Catholics. We have labeled them "transitionals" to emphasize their intermediate position in the framework of the various groupings in the Menomini population. They are not all equally transitional in the sense of moving in any consistent manner toward a more White-oriented cultural position. Though some are so moving, others are occasional participants in native-oriented religious activities. A few have become more or less permanently associated with the Dream Dance, or with Peyotism. This is how these organizations have been maintained.

In the broad sense of the term, most of the Menomini are in transition, though not in a linear transformation, to Whiteman cultural patterns. The members of the native-oriented group have resisted assimilation by reaffirming the validity of the traditional solutions. The Peyotists have synthesized a religion and an ideology that is a kind of encapsulation of the transitional dilemma. The transitionals whom we will describe and interpret in this chapter are those who, at the time we studied them, had not made decisions that brought them back into nativistic groupings or into the acculturated groups.

Transitionals, defined as people who had direct experience with the native-oriented way of life as children but who have moved away from identification with nativistic groupings or organizations and have become Catholic at least in name, are in a decided minority of those under thirty in the present (1970) Menomini population. In the group over thirty, transitionals, if rigorously defined as those with direct experience within nativistic groupings, would still be in the minority. However, given relaxed criteria—simply some form of engagement with

141

native-oriented culture as children and observable movement in some form, during their lifetimes toward a more acculturated way of life—the majority of Menomini are transitional. For most of those under twenty the engagement with native-oriented culture is extremely attenuated, though the children of native-oriented group members, and of Peyotists, who do not stay in these groupings, are transitional in the defined sense of the term.

It is apparent that there are a number of kinds of transitionals in the Menomini population. We will confine our discussion, with the exception of a group of women that we will discuss later, to those people who had experience with the native-oriented culture and who were participants or observers in nativistic groupings (Dream Dance, Medicine Lodge, War Dance, or Peyotism) as children. They are people whose first language was Menomini, though usually the shift to English took place very early—by age five to seven. They are people who have moved away from these identifications and toward a more acculturated status, and who have been baptized Catholic, however nominal this identification may be. The analysis of the transitional examples to follow is relevant, however, to a much larger population among the contemporary Menomini.

Even within this more restricted range, there are a number of different types. By definition, these are people who are in a kind of cultural no-man's-land but who also have available to them elements from more than one culture. It is not surprising that they adapt in various ways. We will therefore study in some depth three individuals, all males, who represent the major types of adaptation we have observed. We will see what they have in common, and what distinguishes them as individuals. We will then discuss briefly the social and psychological adjustments characteristic of the males in our transitional sample as a whole, and locate them in relationship to the other acculturative groupings. We will discuss the transitional women separately, for they do represent quite a different universe than do the males, something we found to be true in all of the acculturative categories.

Though we will provide interpretation and organization, most of the data will be presented by our selected individuals in their own words. We are providing this autobiographical material in some detail because it is crucial to an understanding of transitional adaptation as *experienced*. Without this detail the conflicts as well as the adaptations to them, remain abstractions.[1]

George Ketami

George Ketami lives in town in a large old brick and wood house of six rooms, in fair condition and with modern conveniences. There are several pieces of overstuffed furniture in varying states of repair, and pictures of George Wash-

---

[1] The accounts are condensed from expressive autobiographic interviews collected by George Spindler. The technique was developed by Louise Spindler and used more extensively in her study of the women. See G. Spindler and L. Spindler, "Field Work among the Menomini," in G. Spindler, ed., 1970, and L. Spindler 1962. To protect individuals we have eliminated or changed certain details. Any relationship of personal names or initials to actual living persons is entirely coincidental.

The chain carrier to the master saw in the sawmill.

Inside the mill at Neopit.

ington and several Catholic saints on the walls. His wife is part Chippewa and part White, and they have four children, the oldest nine years old. He works as a master saw operator in the lumbermill. He is interested in politics, and has run for office on an antigovernment, anti-Agency platform. His father became a Peyotist, then a Catholic, but went back to Peyotism. His mother was a nominal Catholic all his life, but was a marginal participant in the *mete·wen*, and then in the Peyote church. George Ketami himself had contact with Peyotism, but he says, "It is bad for the nervous system, deteriorates ambition, and sometimes even kills children—if they come in sick." He says that eating peyote is like eating "dry bark." He has a high school education. He is a great woodsman and fisherman, and provides a significant amount of meat for the family table from woods and streams. He is a tall, slim man, with strong features and an assertive manner.

[You can start any place you wish, it's up to you. Tell it the way you want to.]

I was born just off the reservation right by an old church. I rarely saw my father; I was always practically an orphan. Only on occasions when he wasn't on a log drive or something. I knew I had an older sister but she was never with us. We was never very well to do. I stayed with my grandparents most of the time.

My father joined with the Peyote at the time when we started school. He knew a Winnebago, and he influenced him to join. The only time we saw our parents was when they had a meeting.

I remember, we'd hear them drums when they had a meeting Saturday night. We'd sneak out the window and go to where we heard them drums and we'd find our parents there. They'd have them all special occasions, healing, birthdays, Fourth of July.

An ordinary child couldn't eat that peyote in the raw state. But there was peyote tea—they made us drink that. They used to hold me down. I remember H., and then there was the M. boys, used to make me take it, but only after a fight. It affected you so you couldn't sleep. Straight as an arrow we sat, and listened to those men sing. I guess you might say I was awe stricken. When I was a child you would sort of idolize the certain fellow that sang just right. The peyote would make him sing better as the night progressed. But it didn't seem to have no physical effect on me. We was always given to understand this was medicine.

My dad was about in the same situation I was later; sort of an outcast like. He was baptized in the church; but my mother, she was in Peyote and they sort of dropped him, so he said he would never come back here, for that reason.

Well, I learnt a lot of songs, and so did my brother. We boys used to get together when the regular meeting was over, and sing. The old folks used to think that was pretty good. We tried to imitate the old folks.

[What about school?]

After the first year we went to Keshena school. In those days the government [at Keshena school] tried to make the Indian learn.[2] It was a hard rule, sort of

---

[2] The school at Keshena is no longer run by the Bureau of Indian Affairs and is a public school.

a military life. Absentmindedly, I would talk my own language, and I was severely punished for that. They gave us lickings with a rubber hose. We had to undress for our lickings. I can remember a lot of those. I guess I was ten or eleven years old when I got my first one.

Most of those students were Catholic born, and us who were not Catholic were few in number. There was preachers would come there not of the Catholic faith, and hold little song services for us. Today I can still sing some of those old songs; I can remember them. Naturally there was discrimination. Remarks would be made. It seemed to hit me, more or less. I was hurt by it. My temper was the hair-trigger type.

This school only went as far as the sixth grade. I graduated with high honors. I was twelve then—we got our diplomas and had a big commencement exercise. So during a vacation the police came up to my uncle's and asked me to make application to Haskell Institute.[3] I was working at the time, driving horses for the logs, and I worked in the mill cutting railroad ties, pulling a saw. I remember, I was twelve then. Then I made arrangements to go off to school. Of course, I never wore a suit of clothes before in my life. I worked right up to the time I went to school. My father asked me if I really wanted to go to school. I said, "Sure, my friends is going [school friends], I might as well." My pa wasn't much on education. He couldn't even write. Oh, I guess he could write his name, but that's all. My mother can't write either. So the police took us to the station. They had our tickets ready.

It was the first train ride I ever had; the first time I rode streets cars in Chicago. I never saw a Negro until I was on that train—them porters—I just kept staring at them.

So, I arrived at Haskell. It was a great school, too. It was under military rule—designed like an army camp. The buildings was in a horseshoe, with assignments to them by age. We had commanders like in the army. We marched to and from school and was dismissed from attention. We had a demerit system. If you missed a formation, you was punished on Saturday and required to work all day with no privileges. Those days, newcomers was treated bad. There was different tribes, too—seventy seven of them—Sioux, everything. They was treacherous, so I fought alone. There was other Menomini there, but I was off by myself.

[Why were you off by yourself?]

Because I was a "pagan," and they was Catholic. I was discouraged for a while, but I couldn't run away, it was too far. I was sick. I couldn't eat. The rough treatment was too much. So I took my troubles to the captain. He talked man to man to me. Then things changed, but I was homesick, though I never had a home really. He brought me out of it. I told him I wasn't no better off at home. I had no home. To my mind, that military training helped. It taught me to obey commands, and learn some initiative.

During my years at Haskell I was never a model student. They had a jail

[3] A residential school available to American Indians for advanced, largely vocational education, administered along military lines until very recently, and located at Lawrence, Kansas.

there and I got in it, but for never any offense but misdemeanors—no stealing or nothing like that. We used to write our disciplinarian and explain what happened.

They had football, basketball, anything you could name. Those years they had great teams. We used to idolize those fellows. We had class games—that's where I used to come in—I tried everything. I guess I was just a natural sportsman, an athelete. I was never the best because I was too skinny, but I always made a stab at it.

Those were about the best days of my life. I was there for nine years—from sixth grade up to two years junior college, some courses, anyhow, and finished out with a trade course. I had plans to go to college—but there never was no such thing—it didn't work out.

I never come home during summer. Money problems stopped me, and my parents never together. I never heard from them. I felt I was disowned. I had my own money from the government office and I worked on farms during the summer. Like I say, those were the best years of my life. I took advantage of everything: plays, athletics. Of course I still had that inferiority complex I couldn't erase. It haunted me all the way through. I overcame that somewhat there. Two teachers, especially, helped me. I had one Indian teacher—he knew Indian disposition. He talked me out of it. I had to come out of it. I couldn't speak to even ten people before. He'd make me memorize something and talk to him, and then he'd make me get up before the rest. By the end of the year I could talk good. I know one time we argued, "The only good Indian is a dead Indian." We got pretty hot under the collar about it.

I was twenty when I left there. I never smoked or drank until then. I had intentions of entering the Indian service then, but there was no opening. I landed here in September. I had to get acquainted all over again. I stayed away so long I forgot most of the boys and most of them was married. So I sorta had the blues when I got here. I dunno—I had a funny feeling. The place seemed small to me. I was on the verge of going back. My parents were divorced by that time. The only letter I got at school told me about that.

Well, you know how unemployment affects a person. I had a little money left. I had a lot of fairweather friends and I started drinking—the only recreation around here! I never harmed anybody on my sprees. But, I got picked up and put in jail—my first time in jail here—for possession of liquor. I got ninety days out of it. I was accused on three charges in a kangaroo court with no lawyers. I took the rap for the rest, you might say.

Then when times picked up—I worked here and there, but got laid off every time a married man turned up. I dynamited, sawed logs, made roads, blasted stumps, drove horses, caterpillars, handled lumber, and worked on the log landing. For seven years I worked pretty steady.

People began to take notice of me. They'd sit down, J. P. and them boys, and we'd get into arguments about politics. They said, "Why don't you throw your hat in?" "Oh," I said, "I can't do nothing like that." But I did.

I told my wife, "Now I'm in politics." People got to know me. That fall, elections came. I didn't think I had a chance. I got word next day. J. came to congratulate me. I was surprised. That's how I got my association with J. P. and J. M.—damn nice fellows![4]

So, I served two terms right straight. When there was a tough committee job, J. always put me in it—he'd laugh. Of course, them years we had quite a squabble. Things was going to the dogs. The agent didn't know anything. There was a factional battle and we got him out. Then the people did start to take notice of me. They thought I did good work.

After that I kept out of politics. I had almost forgot how to fish and hunt. That's what I do all my spare time now. My uncle knew all the tricks, like his forefathers did. How to stalk and trap, everything. I learned from him. I got the knack too. I guess you might say it's inherited.

Then finally there was a job open on the master saw. So I grabbed it. Since then I've been working at the saw, and as a foreman, without loss of time. I've realized that if you work steady, every day, and don't shirk, you can't miss.

[The interview was broken at this point, after two and one half hours, and resumed again three days later.]

[Please go on as you were. It is up to you where you want to start. Just tell it your own way.]

My temper always has caused me trouble. There's just one word that always gets me, "pagan." It's caused me lots of trouble. But I always try to remember what my father told me, "Treat your enemies like friends, and you'll find out they are." I always wanted to fight my own battle, with my dukes, but he used to say that if someone abused you that God would take care of them.

For instance, here's something. One time when I was home after I was at Haskell, with my dad, some friends of his came over after supper. They wanted him to go out with them, take his car, and go to a tavern outside to get some liquor and bring back home. I had the keys to his car in my pocket, and he wanted them. I told him, "No, you don't want to go, you won't get back." He says, Ohhhh, yesssss! Sure I will!" "You won't get back in time to go hunting." "Sure, sure. I'll just run down, be back in a few minutes." Well, I gave him the keys and he went off with those fellows.

He was gone a long time, and when he did get back he was all beaten up. His face was cut, his nose bleeding; a pretty beat up old man. What had happened was that them fellows with him wanted to take the car and go off on a real drunk. He wouldn't let them, and he hung onto them keys like they was glued to him. They beat him and kicked him but he fought back as best he could, so they had to give up. Well, one of them boys came by the next day to sort of apologize, I guess. I was mad, and was going to hit him. But my dad got between us and told me, "Now don't do that. God will take care of him. You leave him alone. Don't touch him."

I didn't think nothing of it for a long time. But this fellow went off to war, and then he came back. I heard he was back and that he'd got hurt—a jeep turned over on him [in this country]. After a while he came back to the hos-

---

[4] J. P. and J. M. were both elite acculturated. George Ketami ran for advisory council representative.

pital here. I began to feel sorry for him, even if he was my enemy. So I went to see him one day. I come into his room, and there he was, lying on his stomach, in a cast. He couldn't move nothing but his hands and head. I stood behind his bed a while, looking at him. He didn't even see me, but he sensed my presence, and started crying. Then I walked over to him, "Hello Jim," I said. He could hardly talk.

Well, he was crying because he thought my dad did that to him. You know they believe those old Indians had power to harm people. He thought my dad witched him because he said back then when we almost had that fight that "God will take care of you." I told him, "It can't work that way unless you believe it yourself." My father told me that, too. But, he was sure that he was witched and when he died later a lot of people thought that was what happened.

[What do you really think about it?]

I don't know whether I believe that or not. I guess it's true that it won't work that way unless you believe in it yourself.

[You haven't told me about how you came to meet your wife and get married.]

I'll never forget when I got married. I begun to notice her around town, and one time I talked to her. I could tell after awhile that she thought a lot about me, and we used to meet. Well, I felt like I should come right into the open about it. So after work one night I dressed up, put on a clean shirt, and went over to her house. My knees was shaking and trembling. I knocked on the door. This was the test. If they welcomed me I was in. If they shut the door in my face, I'd know I wasn't wanted. Of course, they knew me, I had been a stumble-bum, a drunk, for awhile after I got out of Haskell, and I wasn't Catholic either. But, I had straightened out pretty well by then and I thought her father was noticing me. He knew I was trying, anyhow. Well, they opened the door, and her ma said, "Come right in. Sit down." Then I knew I was all right. Of course, after that I come regularly, every night—just in time for dishes it seemed, every time. It got to be a joke, and, of course, after awhile we got married, and J. O. has never had a reason to feel ashamed that he took me as a son-in-law.

[A girl brings a little dog that is not being taken care of to him, and he gives her a dime to buy dog food and then says, "That dog may save my life some day."]

You know, there's always some thing that changes the whole course of your life. And J. P. said that one word that changed everything for me. I was out in the hall and I heard him saying, "We can't give him that job—he drinks too much." I came in and asked who he was talking about and he said, "You." I admired him for coming right out in the open and telling me and I told him so, and that changed my whole life.

I became a Catholic when I married to my wife. It has been hard breaking in here. They say the church people are kind and everything but I've had a hard time. Just when I'd begin to think I was one of them, someone would call me a pagan. As first I'd get real mad and fight. But after a while, I kept remembering what my father told me about making friends out of my enemies and it really works.

[Do you go to church much?]

No, I don't go very often. J. P. and those guys are *real* good church people. I can't accept all those things the church teaches and the father and I used to have a lot of long arguments about it.

[Our conversation ended here since he went in to supper. I could not engage him for that evening because he was going to a baseball game. The interview was reopened a week later, with an evening session. He launched directly into his story without prompting from me.]

Thinking over the past, my grandparents trained me, from early babyhood, and that probably accounts for the fact I could get along as I have. It's been one of the traits of the Menomini that they fostered children that was neglected —even White people's children they've taken in like that.

We had to go through certain ceremonies, everything was organized. If you could see this adoption ceremony . . . I was adopted by K. D., you would know. If one loses a child, they look for one of the same age and sex. So D. adopted me. I was the same age as the son he lost. The one that adopts gives gifts to certain persons. They have to treat them as godchildren—like they stand in baptism in the Catholic church. You call them "father," they call you "son." You find that all over here—everybody is bound together somehow, whether a real relationship or not, nobody knows. The old folks used to tell us that—how all the people here was related in some way—a regular network of relationships. Of course, they used to have maybe two or three wives— common law, etcetera—and there was three clans, they used to say, that you was supposed to marry within. Of course, that all broke up when the bands broke up. There was supposed to be three bands in the clan that we were in.

[How old were you when you were adopted?]

I guess I was six or seven when I was adopted. I had to dance behind K. D. —I remember—and do just what he done. I remember they had three drums, in a large circle, with a large entrance from the westerly side. It lasted three days—that was something! Them were quite the days. I barely remember. Oh, they had big days then; the whole community turned out. Everything was well organized. You had to conform to everything to be eligible. That's the thing that struck me about the Menominis. You was brought up and you had to do it; you was so close to it; the things was a must; a part of your life.

[Did you go through the "big dream fast?"]

I wasn't eligible for the *mesaꞏhkatɛwɛꞏw*. I wasn't old enough then. You was marked with a black mark on your forehead and you took bitterroot, for a cleaning-out process at that time. That cleaned you out of every disease. And the fast of three days, all that cleaned you of all past sins, and any disease you might have had. Nowadays they have all sorts of diseases the old Indians never had—gallstones, kidney, ulcers, maybe it was on account of that.

[You see it from both sides. What do you think of Catholicism?]

It's a mystery. Overall, the people in the *metɛꞏwen* [Medicine Lodge] and *niꞏmihɛꞏtwan* [Dream Dance], they consider everybody, Catholic and pagan, alike. They consider there is a Father up above us, a Creator, to whom all peoples refer. There's no difference. What irks us—I don't know where they get the word "pagan." You shudder at the word, because the dictionary definition says a pagan is one who has no religion whatsoever. Personally, I have this opinion—from the narrowminded part of the Catholic church—that's where it stems from. It puts us in a bad spot. It splits the tribe, this discrimination. They don't stop to think what they're saying.

We get into some arguments. The thing is—birth control. We'll take that. The Catholics stress that—there will be no use of drugs or artificial means to prevent children. Many Menomini feel that you can still be a good Catholic and use some form of birth control. That gives the mother a chance to rest up. But the Catholics would have them right along. The old Indians had their own systems. They believed in such a thing as a rest period. They never had such big families. There was only five of us, and that was a large family when I was a kid.

But, the big thing is the discrimination. If you speak your own language they call you pagan, yet the Catholic religion stresses brotherly love. I've been on both sides, and they can't see eye to eye. If these people could understand Menomini, they would get on the inside, then they wouldn't feel that way. Those people at Zoar know their own history without reading it. There's only a few carrying on the old religions now.

It is a blessing that I can talk the language. It's one of the most perfect languages there is. You can express all sorts of things in it you can't in English. I always talk it whenever I get a chance; especially when I want to say something these other guys or a Whiteman can't understand. It's really a comical language, too. Things seem funny in it that would fall flat in English. I never have been ashamed of my language. My children don't speak no more —oh, some little things like po·so·h—to their grandfather. Of course, I can talk some pretty good Chippewa, too.

[How did your father stand?]

Well, my father was sort of ostracized from the Catholics, because he turned Peyote. And when he died, we decided to bury him that way, even though he was baptized Catholic. He always made the statement that he wanted the Peyote people to take him when he died. So they had an all-night session of Peyote, and the next day the Catholic people who come out from town, there was quite a number of them, spoke the rosary for him. There was friends from both sides represented there. Everybody commented on that. It was quite a funeral. It was quite a thing for me—it made me perk up a little. That funeral meeting was the last time I appeared at a Peyote meeting. Oh, no! I was there for my stepmother, too. But, I was never a real participant, just sat in it. Of course, whatever our parents was in, we had to accept in a way.

[Have you ever gone to church much?]

I guess I'm what you'd call one of them lukewarm Catholics. When there is certain requirements such as standing as a godfather, or pallbearer, I'll go. I really haven't had much training in it. The ritual is complicated and I can't really fall into it. Those different things the priest does at the altar, I don't have the least idea what is going on up there. You have to be brought up from parochial school to know all that. I don't know how long it's been since I was at confession, so I'm not eligible for such things as communion. I guess I'm not really converted, yet even. I haven't done what they call Easter duties yet, so the bishop hasn't confirmed me. I better do that someday, something might happen to me, and I'll get thrown into that other cemetery ["potter's field," where persons who are not identified with any religious group are buried].

[He seemed to have exhausted this subject so I switched. "Now, you haven't mentioned anything about sex."]

The old Indians used to follow everything up. If they saw you playing with your dinkie they would tell you the right and wrong things—and watch you right along, always putting a bug in your ear.

I didn't have nothing to do with a girl until I was eighteen. My upbringing was quite strict. When the old people would talk about sex, we had to get out. It was different than now. Our kids stick their noses into everything. It was different in all ways. No child, for instance, ever ate with an adult. There's no control over any kind of behavior, especially sexual behavior, now. There's no guide; these fourteen-year-old girls are easy prey to some sex-minded older fellows. There's illegitimate children all over.

My grandma and my uncle from my mother's side, they was very strict and levelminded. They had principles, and a philosophy. The old man, particularly, used to sit down and talk to us children. The old Indian doctors used to talk over things in front of us. They would take the $M\epsilon^2napos$ stories and give them a moral, like Aesop's fables. I wish I had them down now—like "Why does a skunk stink?" $M\epsilon^2napos$ was behind all them. He was supposed to do superhuman things, and be at the base of practically everything that happened. Some of those stories would make good plots for the comic books now.

I guess that's the way it is. I was raised as an Indian, in the old Menomini way. Then I went off to school and came back only once. Somehow, I couldn't get in with the people in town at all. I had such a lost feeling. It's a chilly feeling that starts from the heart—discouragement. It made me feel that if I could ever get any kind of job outside, that's where I would go, and I prepared myself for that at Haskell when I went back. But, jobs was scarce when I graduated, and there was no work outside—so I've stayed here.

That's the underlying fact that developed my inferiority complex—that I wasn't wanted, having been raised as an Indian, and with my parents in and out the way they were. In Kansas they talked to us about coming back to our people and helping them out with what we learned. But, when I got back here, no one was ready to lend me a hand—it was discouraging.

George Ketami shares much with many other transitional males. The dissolution of the nuclear family and the strong influence of grandparents; the direct though marginal experience with nativistic groupings; the development of acute feelings of marginal identity, isolation, and rejection; punishment for speaking his own language from school authorities and punishment for being a pagan at the hands of his peers. He does not entirely scorn the old ways and is prepared to offer a rational explanation in defense of witchcraft. His early years of experience in the framework of the traditional culture have made a deep mark upon him. He is representative of one adaptation within the transitional population. He adapts by working toward a more acculturated position. He is very aware of his situation and yearns for acceptance. His marriage, his politicking, his steady work on the job, and his expression of attitudes about sex and drinking all denote movement in the same direction—toward an improvement in economic and social status. This improvement in status, given the requirements for acceptance in the elite acculturated group, hastens the acculturation process.

Our next case study is of an individual who has made quite a different kind of adaptation, and yet shares with George Ketami certain features of the transitional experience.

Louie Ke·sek

Louie Ke·sek is a full-blooded Menomini. He lives with his wife and seven children, the oldest of which is eight years old. His home is a one-room shack near the highway several miles from town. The house and surroundings are very littered and badly run down. He carries in his water from a nearby creek. There are no modern conveniences in the house.

He works only to get a short-term "grubstake" or some money for liquor, which he consumes in large quantities as quickly as possible. The family is frequently without food, and all of its members show signs of malnutrition.

He spent one year at a residential Indian school away from home, and went to a local Catholic boarding school to the tenth grade. He had what he regards as a successful navy career for three years. He speaks Menomini poorly, but appears to understand it well.

He is nominally Catholic, but rarely attends services. He is regarded as a Peyotist by some of the members of that group, and has participated in a number of meetings. He is not a member of any other native-oriented ceremonial group, but has his closest associations with their members, and has been marginal to these groups all of his life. His neighbors say he is a man "who don't believe in nothing," a sentiment with which he agrees.

He is tall and thin, and seems undernourished. He spends much of his time sitting in the doorway of his shack. While his person and surroundings appear to be in a condition of nearly absolute physical deterioration, he does not appear depressed.

His parents live in a nearby shack, which is the center of heavy drinking sprees attended by relatives and friends from town. His father is regarded as quite dangerous when drunk, and is a man of uncertain temperament when sober. His father is a member of the ni·mihe·twan (but rarely attends), has been observed inside the lodge at mete·wen ceremonies (but does not possess a medicine bag), and has been a participant in Peyote meetings, but is not considered a reliable member. When the drinking starts on weekends, other Menomini living nearby frequently get in their cars and drive away in order to escape entanglement in the fights that usually start.

He beats his wife when he drinks, and has injured her seriously enough to put her in the hospital. His wife does not hold him responsible for this behavior, nor does he himself, since he "was drinking at the time." He agreed readily enough to being interviewed, but he had to be questioned constantly to keep him going.

Poor housing.

The first thing I remember, I lived by a river. I was the black sheep of the family. I always got left out of everything. My brothers and sisters always got everything they wanted. They didn't take much interest in me. After I got older he [father] changed his mind about it—he always come to me. My brothers and sisters always come to my dad—but I never do.

[Question] I started school when I was six years old. I didn't get much out of it—or I'd have a white-collar job. I went to Keshena. I was glad to go to school. I couldn't wait—I wanted to go right away—my brothers and sisters was all going. It was alright there. It was a boarding school.

[Question] I could speak English before I went to school—I could speak some Menomini too. Every time—they always talked English to me. My mother always talked in English. I was about seventeen when she died. I was close to her. It was just that my dad was kind of mean. I don't know why. I guess he got over it. Whenever I asked for things he never give them to me. I used to get abused. He'd beat me—with a piece of wood—and chase me around.

When I left Keshena then—I went to Haskell. I took a vocational course there, in masonry work. I run away from there. I didn't like it there. It wasn't of my own accord. Another boy from Winnebago got in trouble—asked me to go home from there. I stayed in Nebraska for about six weeks. I wrote home and told 'em where I was and asked for money. They told me not to hook trains any more and sent $35.00. They told me to come home—that I'd freeze to death. I come home two days after that. I bought some clothes—then I come home.

I stayed around Neopit about a week, then I went to that Catholic school at Neopit. I stayed there from the tenth grade, they had no eleventh grade or junior high school. The father there taught beyond that if we wanted to stay and play basketball.

I stuck around then. I didn't move then until I met my wife—she was at Haskell too. We liked each other and got married. I bought a house up here. I still had money in the office then.

[Question] I was in jail for drinkin' about then. I was drinkin' then before that—when I was married. I never did work until I was married. I always had money in the office from an annuity they give us. They held it there until I was old enough.

[Question] I never went into that *mete·wen*. He [father] never had a bag. I never wanted to go into it. I used to go and watch on at the *mete·wen* and the powwow [Dream Dance], but didn't go in. I was baptized Catholic sometime around twelve. My ma wasn't in that either. My grandad on my dad's side was—only once I saw him though. My mother used to talk to me about it.

[Question] When I was in Haskell, I tried to enlist—but I was too skinny —but that was in peacetime. So after the war broke out I was deferred— because I was married, and had children. So I turned right around and volunteered again. I went to the Great Lakes—stayed six weeks and got a nine-day leave—then went to gunnery school in Minnesota for five weeks. Then I went to San Diego and stayed there about five days, I guess. Then I went to Seattle, Washington, and got the ship there to 'Frisco, for about a week. Then we shipped out and went overseas to the Pacific. I was overseas eight months, on a destroyer. I was on the No. 5 gun, 20 mm. I saw a little action out there— got shot at lots of times. It was a good clean life—I got along good with those White fellows. They liked me good.

We used to take that alcohol out of the compasses and mix it with water. There was a lot of women, too. The captain would give us condoms and a little tube to use afterwards. We had to go.

After that fighting, then I came back. As soon as we hit the States we got leave. When my time was up, then I was discharged, at the Great Lakes, an honorable discharge. I was gonna go back to 'Frisco with the Seabees—but I was discharged in '45.

I went back to work in the mill [at Neopit]. I had that musterin'-out pay, but that didn't amount to much. I worked all winter long, then in the spring and summer I'd get out. It was too hot in the mill. I'd pick greens and potatoes —then I'd go back in the mill for the winter.

[Question] I tried the peyote. They always told me it was good—them different ones that used it. I didn't go until I got out of the service—and I haven't gone back much since. [Question] I went to meetings for several years. [Question] Well, about every time they had it—I'd be drinkin'—and I didn't want to go in there when I was drinkin'. [Question] I suppose I got used to drinkin' when I was a kid. I don't know why it is—when I want the money to drink I can get it—but not when I want something else. [Question] I still work in the mill during the winters. I walk in and work nine hours, then walk back again. It's work just walkin' to and from. I used to run that distance when I first got married. [Question] I don't go Catholic much— just on Christmas and Mass—it's about the only time I go. I don't go to nothin'. You go to all them churches to pray. You can go right outside to pray. You can get your answer right outside just as well.

[What about termination?]

If the government leaves us go—I'd get along as a Whiteman alright. I'd go most anyplace. There's different Menominis all over, even in Portland, Oregon. I'd get information from them guys—where they get work. Only thing—I'd have to join a union, I suppose. I'd be better off that way. But most of them guys—they don't know how to get along.

I used to hit the rods all the time—I'd go to different states. In the summertime I wouldn't work. I'd bum meals here and there—whenever the trains stopped.

[Question] I don't know nothin' about witchcraft. No not me. I don't think it can work at all. I don't know if they got witchcraft. I never seen any myself. [Question] No, I never took enough peyote [to have visions]. They say you can see Christ, and that it makes you confess. But I never took enough. I haven't been to a meeting since about three days after my mother died. I went to that meeting where M. D. lives. I started going to them meetings when I was about four years old. My dad was in that, he still uses it sometimes. My dad was baptized in the NAC [Native American Church] since I can remember. [Question] Well, they want him to come over to the powwow [ni·mihe·twan] all the time—they don't baptize them. My ma was in the NAC too—so I guess I was baptized in it. I don't go now. I don't go to nothing.

[Question] No, I never hated Whitemen. I figure my dad was mean against the Whitemen because he never went to school and can't read and write.

[Question] I've got nine brothers and sisters, all from the same mother. [Question] Five brothers. I was the middle one. Three sisters, two older and one younger. K. is my favorite brother. He used to help me out in every way. I'd ask him for money while I was in school—he'd help me out. He was your size about. M. was my favorite sister—the next oldest of sisters. She was the same way as my brother. I used to always fight with them others. They always picked on me—even now, when they're drinkin'—it comes out then—they come out here and fight with me.

[Question] I feel happy now. I'm always happy—there's nothing to worry about. [Question] I don't know what's wrong with the Whiteman. A Whiteman will kill another for money. What good is it? Did you ever hear of an Indian killing for money? [Question] I'm always reading about Whites that do [in newspapers]. [Question] I don't want them [children] to grow up like me. I drink too much. [Question] I got a lot of Whitemen friends—borrow money from them—then have to pay it back! [Question] I go out—pick greens, hunt, fish, sell fish. We went out yesterday—made $9.00 in two hours. When that's gone we'll go out—get some more. No use workin' my head off.

[What's the most important thing that ever happened to you?]

Well, I was across fightin' in the war—when I come back to the States I almost got killed. It wasn't all my fault. My brother-in-law was shootin' at another man. There was two men there, and they got sore and wanted to beat him up. He's a crippled man. I went to help him out and they beat me. I was pretty tight too. He was shootin' at them before with a deer rifle. That's what

I got out of it. First they tried to beat me up—then they tried to run over me. The bumper got me right here [points to knee]. We was all drinkin' and I don't know just what happened. I didn't wake up until next day. I would be layin' there yet if P. T. hadn't come by and picked us up. He got the police on a two-way radio. Just to help somebody out—that's the reward I get!

The major impression one acquires of Louie Ke·sek is that he has little control over his life. He wonders why he can always find money to drink, but not for other things. He has seven ill-fed, inadequately clothed children, and his wife is pregnant again. He is a member of no group. He has no aspirations, and works only to keep alive. His self-estimate is, however, realistic and honest.

The autobiographic interview was difficult for both of us. His replies to questions were laconic, and there is much more that he did not say than he did say. He has no clear identity. He is a Catholic and a Peyotist simultaneously, but participates in neither church.

The rejection, unpredictability, and irascibility of his father is apparently a significant factor in his adjustment. The high point of his life was his stint in the navy. Military experience is often such a high point for Menomini transitionals. The orderly life, and the personal acceptance most Menomini received from White servicemen, made a deep impression.

There are powerful idiosyncratic factors at work in Louie Ke·sek's life pattern. George Ketami also experienced marginality and isolation, but he had a positive relationship with his grandparents to build upon, and he was not abused. Louie Ke·sek has no aspirations. He has such inadequate control over his life circumstances and the instrumental means to change them that he cannot provide for his family. His relations with everyone are defective. He seems unconcerned for the misery in which he and his family live, so much so that he seems almost psychopathic. His Rorschach supports this characterization in part. He produces many sterotypic responses. He sees parts of things that are incidental or irrelevant without any attempt to relate them to each other, or to other aspects of the blots. He produces an above-average number of responses, however, and his responses do not exhibit any gross distortions in perception of structure and form. It would be going too far to call him psychologically ill. He appears to have few skills at relating instrumental activities, such as work, to consistent goals. Indeed, excepting for his time in the Navy, he has had little opportunity to do so.

Acculturation, occurring in the framework we have been describing, is frequently associated with disorder in interpersonal relationships and family life that in turn are reflected in personal apathy and deterioration.

Frank Bear

Frank Bear lives alone in a log cabin, some distance off the main road, that he built himself. He is a full-blooded Menomini, raised by conservative grandparents. He occasionally works in the logging operations, sometimes farms a small garden, and hunts and fishes.